THERE IS NO SUCH THING AS WRITER'S BLOCK

YOU *CAN* UNLOCK YOUR INNER PROLIFIC WRITER

HONORÉE CORDER

AUTHOR, *YOU MUST WRITE A BOOK*

THERE IS NO SUCH THING AS
WRITER'S BLOCK

YOU *CAN* UNLOCK YOUR INNER PROLIFIC WRITER

HONORÉE CORDER

Copyright 2023 © Honorée Enterprises Publishing, LLC

All rights reserved. No part of this book may be reproduced or transmitted in any form or by any means, electronic or mechanical, including photocopying, recording, or by any information storage and retrieval system without written permission of the publisher, except for the inclusion of brief quotations in a review.

Designed by Dino Marino, www.dinomarinodesign.com.

E-book ISBN: 978-1-947665-30-9
Paperback ISBN: 978-1-947665-31-6

ALSO BY HONORÉE CORDER

THE *YOU MUST* BOOK BUSINESS SERIES

- *You Must Write a Book: Boost Your Brand, Get More Business, and Become the Go-To Expert* & *I Must Write My Book: The Companion Workbook to You Must Write a Book*
- *You Must Market Your Book: Increase Your Impact, Sell More Books, and Make More Money* & *I Must Market My Book: The Companion Workbook to You Must Market Your Book*

OTHER WRITING BOOKS

- *Write Your First Nonfiction Book: A Primer for Aspiring Authors*
- *The Bestselling Book Formula: Write a Book that Will Make You a Fortune* & *The Bestselling Book Formula Journal*
- The *Like a Boss* Book Series
- *The Miracle Morning for Writers* with Hal Elrod & Steve Scott
- The *Prosperity for Writers* Book Series

OTHER BOOKS & SERIES

- *Business Dating: Applying Relationship Rules in Business for Ultimate Success*
- *Stop Trying So F*cking Hard: Live Authentically, Design a Life You Love, and Be Happy (Finally)*
- *Tall Order: Organize Your Life and Double Your Success in Half the Time*
- *Vision to Reality: How Short-Term Massive Action Equals Long Term Maximum Results*
- *The Divorced Phoenix: Rising from the Ashes of a Broken Marriage*
- *If Divorce is a Game, These are the Rules: 8 Rules for Thriving Before, During and After Divorce*
- *The Miracle Morning* Book Series with Hal Elrod
- *The Successful Single Mom Book Series*

SPECIAL INVITATION

Be sure to sign up for instant access to all of the resources and bonuses included in this book:

HonoreeCorder.com/JustWrite

DEDICATION

This book is dedicated to my beloved kitty, Sylvester Pickles, Esq., who was an example of pure love, kindness, and personality.
RIP, Mr. Pickles.

We miss you, buddy.

TABLE OF CONTENTS

INTRODUCTION i

CHAPTER ONE
**A BRIEF HISTORY OF WRITER'S BLOCK
(AND WHY YOU DON'T NEED IT)** 1

CHAPTER TWO
PROFESSIONAL WRITERS JUST WRITE 8

CHAPTER THREE
WHAT'S REALLY BLOCKING YOU? 21

CHAPTER FOUR
REMOVE THE BLOCK(S) AND BUILD ANEW 32

CHAPTER FIVE
**BECOME THE WRITER YOU'VE
ALWAYS KNOWN YOU COULD BE** 46

CHAPTER SIX
CLEAR THE DECKS & SET THE (WRITING) STAGE 62

CHAPTER SEVEN
SURROUND YOURSELF WITH OTHER WRITERS 89

CHAPTER EIGHT
LET THOSE WORDS FLOW, NOW AND FOREVER 112

AUTHOR'S NOTES 128

PLEASE REVIEW THIS BOOK 132

GRATITUDE 133

WHO IS HONORÉE CORDER? 134

INTRODUCTION

Hello, Reader!

It's so cool of you to pick up this book. I'm curious—are you reading this because you want to believe there's no writer's block? Or you want to eliminate yours for good? Or maybe because you can't believe I don't think there *is* writer's block?

I'd love to know, so please go ahead and send me an email: <u>Honoree@HonoreeCorder.com</u>. I hope it's the beginning of an awesome, long-term conversation between us.

Now, let's talk about writer's block. Obviously, there is such a thing, or it wouldn't have a name. Right? Right.

However.

In my experience, and I've had a lot of experience, there's really no reason for any writer to have writer's block. I don't have it. I've never had it, and I can give some reasons for that fact. Most of the professional writers I know don't have it, and many don't believe in it!

And, in this book, I will show you how to get rid of it if you think you've got it. Plus, I'm going to help you to never experience it ever again.

That's a big promise, and I promise to deliver.

Note: If you don't have writer's block, there's no need for you to get it. Skip to Chapters Five through Eight to learn some ways to crank your word count into high gear.

Have you ever heard of chef's block, flight captain's block, or garbage collector's block?

Of course not. Imagine you were onboard an aircraft, as I am at this moment, and the captain came over the loudspeaker and said, "Hey, y'all, I'd really love to fly this plane, but I *just can't even* today." What would you do? (Can you imagine?)

Would you say, "Yeah, okay, buddy, go on and hit the lounge. Don't mind us and our intended destination. We're all good! Take a nap. Binge on some Netflix. We'll chill until you're into it."

Noooooo.

You'd be white hot like I've seen some delayed travelers today, demanding Captain Excuses pull up those big kid britches and fly the flippin' plane.

Right? Yup, right again.

Somewhere along the way (I talk about this in-depth in Chapter One), you might have gotten the idea that writer's block was a thing *for you* and allowed that potent power of suggestion to invite you to dance.

You might have hit a brick wall, where one minute the words were flowing, and the next minute they didn't come. And you thought, Oh, I must have writer's block. *OH NO! I have writer's block!*

And you did what others shared they do when they have writer's block. Procrastinated. Watched television. *Talked* about your writer's block.

Lord have mercy; you might have even gone on Facebook and found other blocked writers. Of course, misery loves company, so the minute you mentioned it, other writers jumped on that bandwagon.

"I've got writer's block. Anyone else?"

"Girl, you know it! I haven't been able to write for weeks!"

"Yeah, I'm blocked, too. Binged on Game of Thrones. Have you seen it?"

"Doesn't everyone have writer's block? I've been working on my book for three years!"

You were stuck. Maybe you *are* stuck. You're not sure what to do, so you found this book, hoping it could help.

Well, I've got you. I wrote it because, for the love of all that's holy, I want writers to do what they love to do: *write*.

Write with abandon.

Write the words as fast as they flow.

Write because it is what they—you—were born to do.

Write for a living—a great living!

Which means we've got work to do.

"Writer's block is my unconscious mind telling me that something I've just written is either unbelievable or unimportant to me, and I solve it by going back and reinventing some part of what I've already written so that when I write it again, it is believable and interesting to me. Then I can go on. Writer's block is never solved by forcing oneself to 'write through it,' because you haven't solved the problem that caused your unconscious mind to rebel against the story, so it still won't work— for you or for the reader."

—Orson Scott Card

CHAPTER ONE

A BRIEF HISTORY OF WRITER'S BLOCK (AND WHY YOU DON'T NEED IT)

What if you'd never heard of writer's block? *What if* when you sit down to write, the words flow from your fingers as if by magic?

Can you imagine a world where you write prolifically, continuously, and ceaselessly? Please do. *I want you to!*

Is it possible to always—or almost always—have an unending flow of words at the exact time you need them?

I believe the answer is yes. I know it's an unpopular opinion. Writer's block doesn't exist—and yet, here we are, having this as-yet and still one-sided conversation.

In my experience, and in the experience of dozens, nay, hundreds of writers I know personally, writer's block is not a thing.

In my research for this book, I read an article that proclaimed, "Writers will say they have no writer's block, but in hushed tones, admit they do."

I say the opposite is also true. Writers will say, "Sure, writer's block is a thing, but not for me. When I sit down to write, I write."

I have the same experience. When I sit down to write, I write. The words flow until I run out of time to write. I run out of time, not words.

Well, sometimes I run out of brain power, but that's not writer's block.

I know how I got here, and in every single chapter of this book, I'm going to do my best to help you get here, too. Let's get into it, so you can get out of it.

What's the difference between those who have it and those who don't? Great question, if I do say so myself. The difference starts with understanding, and an understanding leads to a new belief. New beliefs lead to new behaviors, and new behaviors lead to new outcomes.

In order to break free from something—anything—that's holding us back, understanding it can help immensely. When we understand a block (yes, including writer's block), and see it for what it is, very often, we can leave it behind.

Writer's block seems dark and heavy, holding back otherwise brilliant creators from writing all they can write and being all they can be.

I think it's time to shine a light on that dark place and illuminate it forever. I've done it, and so can you.

Let's jump into the Wayback Machine for a few, shall we?

Most people are aware of the psychosomatic condition known as hypochondria, where an individual has a preoccupying fear they have a serious medical condition despite proper medical evaluations and assurances that their health is, indeed, fine.

What you might not have heard about is Medical Student Syndrome. Medical school students frequently report experiencing the symptoms of the diseases they are studying.

Dr. Bernard Baars, in his book *In the Theater of Consciousness: The Workspace of the Mind*, wrote:

"Suggestible states are very commonplace. Medical students who study frightening diseases for the first time routinely develop vivid delusions of having the 'disease of the week'—whatever they are currently studying. This temporary kind of hypochondria is so common that it has acquired a name, 'medical student syndrome.'"

In 1947, Dr. Edmund Bergler, who was then a famous Austrian psychiatrist living in New York City, coined the term "writer's block." And while I'm not sure exactly how a nonmedical condition became a pervasive belief in today's culture, it appeared to rise in popularity in conjunction with the sudden prestige of psychiatry. Hmm. Interesting, right?

It appears as though the power of suggestion had a huge part to play and, frankly, still has a stranglehold today. Even though some writers who never experience it fully accept it exists, I want to challenge it at its very core.

In the introduction, I suggested we wouldn't accept blocks in other professions. We wouldn't co-sign pilot's block, accountant's block, or mechanic's block. There could be no mail carrier's block, Amazon delivery driver's block, or waiter's block. In fact, as a society, we expect, almost require, instant gratification in as many instances as possible at that!

And yet writer's block remains, taking unsuspecting and unempowered writers down with it. It even wields so much power that it has several nicknames, including "noonday devil" and "midnight disease."

Enough! I say! *Enough.*

I've written this to empower you to understand writer's block for what it is (and what it isn't). To inspire you to write—for the first time or forever. And to embolden you to write, just write because it is what you're called to do.

You want to write. I want you to write. I believe you can, and I want you to believe you can. I'm so ready. I have a feeling you are, too!

The first order of business is to challenge your assumption and, therefore, your belief. What if you didn't have writer's block? What possibilities would open up for you?

Next, it is important to keep these three things in mind:

One. It is possible to prevent or reduce the number, strength, and severity of your instances of writer's block.

Two. There are specific ways to break through any block when it occurs.

Three. You can effectively remove every variety of writer's, or even creative, block.

You just need to crack your writer's code.

In this book, I'm going to help you do that. First, by helping you to wrap your arms around your writing. Second, at the close of each chapter, I've created an exercise you can do to help you on your writer's block-free journey.

Be sure to keep your journal handy so you can do these exercises as you complete each chapter. Alternatively, I've created a companion to this book (the *I Am a Writer! Notebook*). Let's begin with the first exercise; it's awaiting you on the next page.

CHAPTER ONE EXERCISE

Answer the questions:
- Do I believe in writer's block?
- Do I believe I sometimes have writer's block?
- What would be possible in my life and career if I didn't have writer's block?

CHAPTER TWO

PROFESSIONAL WRITERS JUST WRITE

With any luck, I've sparked the hope you might always be ready to write. But if you're still staring at a blank page or a blinking cursor, I understand. A little empowerment sometimes only goes so far.

As someone who regularly questions her assumptions, I started questioning mine on writer's block long ago. I'm often asked, "How do you feel about writer's block?" Or, "Do you ever experience writer's block?" And, "Do you believe in writer's block?"

My answers have always been, *I don't think it exists; it doesn't exist for me. No.* And, *No.*

I decided a long time ago, even before writing a book was on my radar, that I must be able to write when I need to write.

I'm not one to seek struggle. In fact, I kinda like the path of least resistance. I decided that whenever I sat down to write something—and initially, it was the emails that later became the basis for my newsletters—I could write.

No block. No problem.

In fact, I firmly believe I should be able to write as soon as I sit at the computer. Instantly, without any warm-up and no need to "get in the mood," I pour words onto the page at a breakneck pace. I knew—and know—the only way to sustain such a prolific pace is to always be able to write whenever and wherever I am. I've also decided I simply can't afford to *not* be able to write.

To start, I've adopted the belief system that I am boundlessly creative, with vast memory banks of information and experience, and can sit down and have words pour out of me as fast as I can type them. I know when I need them, the juices—ideas and words—will flow. This belief allows me to approach my writing projects in a completely relaxed, confident state so I can function at peak performance levels. I don't have time for any type of block. When I sit down to write, I write.

So do I believe writer's block exists? Sure. But I'm not entirely convinced it needs to. And if it does need to, it doesn't need to exist for me. I want you to believe it doesn't need to exist for you, either.

If this is the very first moment you've heard something like this, you might think, *I'd love that to be me*. May I suggest you simply say, "I like that for me, too! Sounds great! Adopted!" Please don't overthink it; you can think this is a solid idea, assume it is true, and proceed accordingly.

And yet, I know you might need *more*, as the thought of just "adopting a belief" might not be enough. I understand.

Is it possible the power of suggestion entered your writing picture at an opportune moment? You might have been working on something in between periods of flow, and someone said,

"I bet you have writer's block."

Perfect timing, imperfect suggestion.

Think back. When was the first time you thought you had writer's block? When was the first time it was suggested to you?

My questions here can create cognitive dissonance—to help you start to challenge your belief in writer's block. Not necessarily about whether you believe in it or you don't, but to question whether you need to have it.

I'm going to use The Buddha's Story of the Angry Man here as an example:

> One day, Buddha was walking through a village. A furious young man came up and began insulting him. "You have no right teaching others," he shouted. "You are as stupid as everyone else. You are nothing but a fake."
>
> Buddha was not upset by these insults. Instead, he asked the young man, "Tell me, if you buy a gift for someone, and that person does not take it, to whom does the gift belong?"
>
> The man was surprised to be asked such a strange question and answered, "It would belong to me, because I bought the gift."
>
> The Buddha smiled and said, "That is correct."

And it is exactly the same with your anger.

If you become angry with me and I do not get insulted, then the anger falls back on you.

What if you returned the "gift" of writer's block to the giver? Can you give it back? What if you, instead, "returned to sender"?

Most likely you're a professional and using some kind of block as an excuse for not completing an aspect of your work has never occurred to you. You're a pro, and pros get the job done. You show up to work when you feel like it, and you work. You show up to work when you don't feel like it, and you work.

Writing is virtually no different. When a professional writer needs to write something, with little or no delay, they write. I said *virtually* because I acknowledge the creative aspect of writing. Professional writers aren't special; they weren't born under a special star and don't have a unique and unattainable talent. That might be hard to believe right at this moment but stay with me here.

Now some say creativity cannot be forced—however, I believe we can engineer circumstances to ensure writing productivity on demand. Yes, just like the pros do.

When my daily morning writing alarm sounds, I sit down to write, and I write. It really is as simple as that. I have a deadline for this book, and there's no reason I won't hit it. Not one.

And I am certainly not the only writer like this.

I don't believe I'm special, a prolific unicorn with unique powers. I've cracked my code with a combination of effective beliefs, an understanding of how I work at my best, and a firm commitment to doing the work.

No, that answer isn't sexy. It's not exciting. But the result is the book you hold in your hands.

Many famous writers have shared their thoughts on writer's block, some funny, some insightful. Here are a few:

"Writer's block is a fancy term made up by whiners, so they have an excuse to drink alcohol." –Steve Martin

"There's no such thing as writer's block. That was invented by people in California who couldn't write." –Terry Pratchett

"Writer's block is simply the dread that you're going to write something horrible. But as a writer, I believe that if you sit down at the keys long enough, sooner or later something will come out." –Roy Blount, Jr.

"Writer's Block—when your imaginary friends stop talking to you." –Eva Dane

"I learned to produce whether I wanted to or not. It would be easy to say oh, I have writer's block, oh, I have to wait for my muse. I don't. Chain that muse to your desk and get the job done." –Barbara Kingsolver

"Writer's block… a lot of howling nonsense would be avoided if, in every sentence containing the word WRITER, that word was taken out and the word PLUMBER substituted; and the result examined for the sense it makes. Do plumbers get plumber's block? What would you think of a plumber who used that as an excuse not to do any work that day?

The fact is that writing is hard work, and sometimes you don't want to do it, and you can't think of what to write next, and you're fed up with the whole damn business. Do you think plumbers don't feel like that about their work from time to time? Of course, there will be days when the stuff is not flowing freely. What you do then is MAKE IT UP. I like the reply of the composer Shostakovich to a student who complained that he couldn't find a theme for his second movement. "Never mind the theme! Just write the movement!" he said.

Writer's block is a condition that affects amateurs and people who aren't serious about writing. So is the opposite, namely inspiration, which amateurs are also very fond of. Putting it another way: a professional writer is someone who writes just as well when they're not inspired as when they are." –Philip Pullman

"You can't think yourself out of a writing block; you have to write yourself out of a thinking block." –John Rogers

"It's not the fear of writing that blocks people. It's the fear of not writing well; something quite different." –Scott Berkun

Whether pros believe in it or not, when it is time to write, it is time to write, simple as that.

"Over the years, I've found one rule. It is the only one I give on those occasions when I talk about writing. It's a simple rule. If you tell yourself you are going to be at your desk tomorrow, you are by that declaration asking your unconscious to prepare the material. You are, in effect, contracting to pick up such valuables at a given time. Count on me, you are saying to a few forces below: I will be there to write." –Norman Mailer in *The Spooky Art: Some Thoughts on Writing*

Yes, plenty of other writers have become famous for their writer's block. They discuss writing more than they actually write, which results in missed deadlines, less or no income, and painful anxiety.

To me, that sounds awful. I'm not putting any of those folks in here because I know keeping your mind open to new possibilities will get you into the flow of writing faster than anything else you could do.

Allow me to use the power of suggestion here, with the intention of good:

You are a writer. When you sit down to write, regardless of the time of day, location, day of the week, your age, how much sleep you got last night (or didn't), and what's going on around you, you write.

Professionals write when it's time to write. I know I said that, and I believe it bears repeating. Plus, there's more.

- Professionals believe when it's time to write, whether they have an internal or external deadline, they write.

- Professionals know you can't edit a blank page, so they fearlessly write a first draft. They know an editor (or more than one editor *and* a proofreader) will come behind them to make their writing shine.
- Professionals are fine to sit, waiting for the words to flow while they compose their thoughts. In fact, they expect there to be a fair amount of space in between the words—and in between times of flow.

Professional writers pay attention to what works for them with their writing—and soon, you will, too.

This book will equip you with the tools and strategies you need to write more prolifically and faster than you ever dreamed possible.

It is possible. It is possible for *you*.

You are not alone! If you need to know there are plenty of successful, professional writers *who are just like you* writing when they need to write, here are some examples:

- Tonya Kappes, a prolific cozy mystery writer, said, "I don't believe in it. If you're stuck, then you wrote something that needs to be fixed. Go back and reread what you've written. It will reveal itself to you." Tonya publishes *one book per month* and is approaching the two-hundred-book mark as I write this.

- "Walking helps me." –Sherri Hughes Gragg, nationally published and award-winning freelance writer.
- Nurse, retired paramedic, and prolific author Jamie Davis shared, "Write about something mundane in the scene until the words start flowing again on target. I call it making a sandwich. In a kitchen, write about a character making a sandwich. In a garden, plant a flower. And so on. It's worked for me many times."
- "Writer's block is a sign your story is going in the wrong direction." –J. T. Ellison, thriller writer, cat lover, friend.

Have you embraced the belief I suggested? Perhaps writing it on a 3x5 card and reading it a few times a day will help you digest it and *own it.*

Then, do the Chapter Two exercise before you keep reading. These two action steps combined will help adjust your course on the journey to prolific, professional writer.

CHAPTER TWO EXERCISE

Turn on your brain's reticular activating system (RAS): look for writers you know who write easily and prolifically. Make your list then add to it every time you find someone new!

I promise that by identifying these kinds of writers, you will feel empowered to own your ability to write easily and prolifically.

"Many years ago, I met John Steinbeck at a party in Sag Harbor, and told him that I had writer's block. And he said something which I've always remembered, and which works. He said, 'Pretend that you're writing not to your editor or to an audience or to a readership, but to someone close, like your sister, or your mother, or someone that you like.' And at the time I was enamored of Jean Seberg, the actress, and I had to write an article about taking Marianne Moore to a baseball game, and I started it off, 'Dear Jean, . . .' and wrote this piece with some ease, I must say. And to my astonishment that's the way it appeared in Harper's Magazine. 'Dear Jean, . . .' Which surprised her, I think, and me, and very likely Marianne Moore."

—John Steinbeck by way of George Plimpton

CHAPTER THREE

WHAT'S REALLY BLOCKING YOU?

"Things are going to get real—really fast." That's what my trainer says when we start the third set of twelve reps—when my shoulders protest the amount of weight I'm pressing over my head, the muscles threatening to give up at precisely the wrong moment.

Right after things get real, when I feel like I want to, must, or should stop, this is the point where I must commit to continue pressing.

You may believe in writer's block and attribute your lack of writing to it.

You might say, "Writers get writer's block. It's a fact."

Perhaps you've been making excuses for not finishing that first, or final, draft. You blame writer's block, and why wouldn't you? It's been so often cited as the culprit for others. What else could it be? Why wouldn't it be the case for you?

Maybe you haven't called it writer's block, per se, but feel your situation might be a close relative. You haven't been able to find the right words. You've been busy—when would you fit writing in? After all, you've got so many other things to do. You would write, but finding enough time to do your project justice is a challenge.

All reasonable—and just about anyone would hear you, nod, smile, and co-sign your (ahem) *bullshit*.

I know because I have said or done all of those.

They are fine excuses, of course. *But they aren't writer's block.*

What if your lack of writing isn't writer's block but something else entirely?

What if the reasons you're not writing are something you can overcome, and sooner than later, be in the flow of writing, easy like Sunday morning? Wouldn't that be great? (It would!)

So if it's not writer's block, what is it? And how can you fix it? *I'm glad you've asked.*

WHAT'S REALLY BLOCKING YOU?

Would you be shocked, surprised, or even offended if I said your block is *you*?

Again, stay with me.

My friend and Empire Builders Mastermind member, business mentor Helen Bullen, is kindly blunt. I'm going to borrow Helen's British ways for a moment and say you are standing squarely in your own way. Whether or not you know it, you are most likely your biggest problem.

Before you stop reading and close the book—maybe forever—please hear me out. *I am here as a friendly.* I want, more than anything, for you to be writing. You do, too, right?

This is the elephant in the room. If you're not writing, it most likely comes down to a few things: beliefs, behaviors, and time.

Yes, it could be something else, but these seem to be the prime offenders. Note: If you do have something deeper going on (such as unresolved trauma), I encourage you to do whatever is necessary to get to the other side. The work to get there can frankly *suck* (I know this from personal experience), and it is entirely worth it.

The good news is your beliefs, behaviors, or time limitations aren't permanent. They can be altered, reversed, or eliminated, leaving the way clear for you to *just write whenever and wherever you sit down to write.*

With some inner work and self-reflection, I know you can step out of your own way and set yourself up to be something akin to a writing machine.

This chapter discusses actual writing blocks. Later chapters will guide you to overcome them and become a writing force to be reckoned with.

Imagine being able to write as much as you want, anytime you'd like. Instant creativity! Words on demand! Sounds delightful, right? It is (and it is fun, too)! Let's get you there as soon as possible.

IT MIGHT NOT BE WRITER'S BLOCK. IT COULD BE ...

Let's explore these three alternatives for writer's block, one at a time: *belief block*, *behavior block*, and *time block*.

Belief Block. Personal beliefs are foundational to success—in writing or just about anything (creative or otherwise). We can hold beliefs in either direction—something is possible or impossible.

Chances are high you have a belief that doesn't serve you (or help you write).

The alternate theory here? You just might have "belief block."

You may have the belief "it's not possible to write on demand." Or, "I have writer's block; it's impossible for me to write."

Perhaps you have conditional beliefs about writing. If you believe you can write only under certain circumstances—"I must be facing east at noon on Tuesdays during months ending in "r" with a vanilla-scented candle burning and coffee heated to 128 degrees—*then* and only then will the words come"—any other time, it stands to reason you'll be unable to write. That, of course, is ridiculous—as I'm sure you can see—but perhaps you have a belief that could be a distant relative?

Alternatively, you might believe you don't deserve to be a writer or be paid well for the words you've written. Your belief block might stem from feeling like you're an imposter, or it's been intensified because you're a perfectionist.

What do you believe? Because if you believe in writer's block, you're more likely to have it. If you don't believe in writer's block (or, as I do, that if it exists, I surely never have it), you're less likely to experience it.

Behavior Block. Writing is a behavior. Not writing is, regardless of cause, a (lack of) behavior.

Behaviors are, of course, driven by beliefs. When you believe you can do something, your behaviors reflect those beliefs. The opposite is also true.

What writing behaviors are you engaging in, or failing to engage in? Or have you simply leaned so far into your belief in writer's block that you haven't even tried to write? Have you made a writing appointment and showed up, or did you just go on about your business, leaving that elephant to fend for itself?

Hey, I'm not calling you out. I'm simply asking. I want you to figure this out, and as Marie Forleo says, "Everything is figureoutable." We're going to sort this out together and get you writing.

Here's something fun to note: You can behave your way into a new belief. You can change your beliefs by acting despite fear or doubt. "I know I have writer's block, but I'm going to sit down and write a few words anyway. Let's see what happens."

Said another way, you can prove it to yourself by actually doing it.

I'm sure you've done something scary or completely out of your comfort zone and afterward thought, *That wasn't so bad.* Or maybe you just completely shifted into the most outstanding version of yourself and said, *Yeah, I'm a badass. I always knew I could do it.*

Maybe, just maybe, your beliefs are fine. You're a writer, and you know it. You can write when you sit down to write. Then what is really at the bottom of all this not writing business?

Time Block. Some writers have plenty of time. Too much time, in fact. I've met my fair share of those who have hours and hours every day to write, and yet they just *aren't*. Some soul's days are booked end to end, leaving little or no time to write.

If you've got a lot of time to write, that could be your problem. You've found yourself with time, or blocked it off to write, yet even given the ideal circumstances, the words do not come. Perhaps you have no deadline—self-imposed or external—to get you *on* your ass and writing.

You might be a busy professional or entrepreneur, a full-time parent (or both), and the list of things to do is endless. Where would you fit in time to write? I get it.

I am or have been all of those during my writing career, which is why I had to figure it out.

You'll notice I am not yet offering suggestions or solutions. This is all by design because in order to progress from a trickle to a flood, it's important to first shine a light in the dark place.

Before we continue, please take a moment to consider which of the three blocks—belief, behavior, or time—apply to you.

What? You've got some of all three? Congratulations! No, I'm serious—the first step is to identify the challenge. You're in the right place. In short order, we're going to move you from a dribble to a gush—from almost no words to *all the words*.

Come with me now; we've got some blocks to remove!

CHAPTER THREE EXERCISE

Which block—*belief*, *behavior*, or *time*—is holding you back?

What is the first thing that comes to mind that could help you overcome it?

"If you get stuck, get away from your desk. Take a walk, take a bath, go to sleep, make a pie, draw, listen to music, meditate, exercise; whatever you do, don't just stick there scowling at the problem. But don't make telephone calls or go to a party; if you do, other people's words will pour in where your lost words should be. Open a gap for them, create a space. Be patient."

—Hilary Mantel

CHAPTER FOUR

REMOVE THE BLOCK(S) AND BUILD ANEW

I can (almost) hear you in my head as I'm writing.

Wait, that's it? Identify blocks and move on?

Just about. I've got a process for eliminating problems, challenges, issues—whatever you want to call them—and it doesn't include a ton of overthinking.

Don't we already *know* the problem?

Problem: You are not writing.

Additional problem: You might be overthinking *the problem*.

Additional problem: You might also be asking yourself ineffective questions.

Overthinking and worrying about writing can lead to a vicious cycle of not making progress. There's no beginning, and no end, and certainly no actual *writing*.

Amid all of this uncertainty, it is quite possible you're asking yourself some questions.

As my mother says, "Ask a silly question, get a silly answer."

I assumed if I wasn't careful, the question I was asking wouldn't get me the answer I really wanted. Nor would it get me closer to any sort of valuable solution. Or, I might get a brilliant answer but to the wrong question.

"Give me an example, Honorée."

Of course. I thought you'd never ask.

Are you asking questions about your writing, such as:

"How am I ever going to get this done?"

"Why am I still blocked?"

"Who am I to write a book (articles, dissertation, proposal, screenplay, hit song, etc.)?"

"Hasn't someone covered everything about this topic in their writing?"

"Is this even good... *at all?*"

"No one makes money from writing, do they?"

"Am I even a writer?"

Let's try something new—something that can work wonders for this or any obstacle in your path from this day forward. A tall order. A big promise. I've got you on this because I've got the miles, silver hair, and results to show for them.

> *"Whether you think you can,*
> *or you think you can't—you're right!"*
>
> –Henry Ford

EFFECTIVELY QUESTION EVERYTHING

Challenge, Then Change, Your Questions

It might be time to call your beliefs into question and challenge your assumptions. I want you to question your beliefs and assumptions—and when you discover the ones that don't serve you, *replace them with ones that do.*

- *Is it true* you don't deserve to make money as a writer?

- *Is it true* you can't find the time to write?

- *Is it true* you don't have a solid idea?
- *Why can't you* write?
- *Why won't* the words come?
- *Who are you* to be a writer anyway?

Instead of wondering whether the questions are "right" or "wrong," "good" or "bad," focus on whether something is *effective* or *ineffective*.

Those questions are ineffective. Why? Because when you ask a question, you get an answer! Your brain is actually a powerful (and much underused) computer, and it will spit out answers to any question you ask of it. Kind of like the artificial intelligence (AI) everyone freaks out about, only sometimes it's ineffective and not nice.

Maybe these answers to the questions above will sound familiar:

- Probably. Who makes money as a writer anyway?
- You're too busy to write. Give it up, Buster.
- Your idea sucks.
- You can't write because you're not a writer. Duh.
- The words won't come, because see the previous answer.

- You're not a writer. We've discussed this. Get an actual job.

Yeah, that computer you've got on your shoulders can be a real jerk. #rude

Perhaps it's not the computer. Let's craft some more effective questions, shall we?

How about:

- *Is it true* you deserve to make money as a writer?
- *Is it true* you can carve out the time to write?
- *Is it true* you have so many solid ideas?
- *Why am I* a writer? Or *Why am I* always able to write when it's time to write?
- *Why is it so easy* for the words to come?
- *Who am I* to do anything else besides being a writer?

Which leads that voice in your head to new, awesome answers:

- *Yes! I absolutely deserve to make money as a writer!*
- *Yes, I write in big chunks and small pieces. It's amazing!*
- *Yes, so many ideas! All ideas, all the time.*

- *Because I was born to be a writer!* Or, *Writers write when it's time to write! (Obviously.)*
- *It's easy for me to write because I am a writer, and I love to write.*
- *It wouldn't make sense for me to be anything other than a darn good writer because that's what I am.*

I'm sure you can see and maybe even feel how good questions lead to ingenious answers—and glorious feelings. Yes, it really is just that simple: to look at your most asked questions and then see whether the answers empower and inspire you (or whether the opposite is true).

SUSPEND DISBELIEF

Before you can truly engage in changing a belief behind which all words will flow, it's helpful to suspend disbelief. Kind of like when you watch those John Wick movies or just about any action thriller.

There's *no way* one guy is going to take down a whole slew of bad guys and come out with just a mildly bleeding scratch on his temple. *Impossible.* But is it possible?

Create cognitive dissonance, the mental discomfort that comes from holding two conflicting beliefs or attitudes. This is happening right now because you have "new" information: there's no such thing as writer's block.

Then you have two choices: you can defend your position. "Yes, there is Honorée, and here's your book back—not recommended!" Or, you can challenge your assumption and change your belief. This is the one I recommend, although I'm sure that's obvious.

Allow me to help by asking you a question of my own:

WHAT IS YOUR BLOCK COSTING YOU?

Seriously, what is it costing you to believe in writer's block, or not to believe you deserve to be a writer who makes a great income and feels worthy of sharing your words with the world?

Possibly, a whole metric ton of good things.

The impact your writing is *not* making.

The income your writing is *not* bringing in.

The lack of creativity in your life and/or business.

The opportunity for you to become the writer, no, the *writing professional* you've always dreamed of being.

Well, darn. This is a huge bummer.

I don't know what my life would be like if I hadn't taken the advice to write a book and run with it. I certainly don't think I'd be writing these words here today. I'd miss out on relationships, royalties, and so much more.

It makes me momentarily sad to think about it until I realize I'm sitting here at my desk at 8:13 a.m. writing this to you. I hope you'll replace your limiting belief and someday send me a handwritten note (I do love a handwritten note). I'd love to hear that your screenplay became a movie or that magazines around the world feature your articles. Or you wrote "The End" on the last page of your first draft. Or . . . insert the writing goal you've had for quite some time and achieved it. *This is gonna be so cool!*

Gosh darn it, *please*, for the love of all that's holy and possible, get clear on what your block is costing you. Then get clear with the knowing you need to get rid of that block, change your beliefs, and get to writing!

"But how do I do that, Honorée?" Yes, I hear you. Let's continue.

CHALLENGE, THEN CHANGE, YOUR BELIEFS

Is it possible you can proceed without writer's block? Is it possible you could challenge any beliefs that don't serve you, and perhaps replace them with some that do?

Say it with me: "*Yes!*"

Is it effective to believe you don't deserve to make money as a writer, that you don't have time to write, or your ideas aren't solid?

Say this with me, too: "*No!*"

Of course it's not, and I think deep down inside, you truly know this. You know, being down on yourself, wading in a pool of self-doubt, and not putting words on the page isn't for your highest and best good.

The change in questions might help. But when you're stuck, and you've answered some of those original questions (and gotten the answers that leave you stuck), you might not be in the place to make a change.

I understand. You may be inspired by what you've read so far but don't know how to get unstuck. I've got you. Let's get you unstuck.

FIRST, THE CHALLENGE, THEN THE CHANGE

Here's an exercise you can do, solo or in a group setting, to help you challenge and then change your beliefs. I learned this as a student of Tony Robbins, and this is his process:

1. Identify the belief.
2. Take 100 percent responsibility.
3. Let go of certainty.
4. Change your self-talk.

IDENTIFY THE BELIEF

Most likely, your belief is something like one of the questions above:

- I don't deserve to be a writer.
- I'm not a good enough writer.
- I can't make money as a writer.

What belief is holding you back from being your highest and best self—as a writer—and therefore, you're not writing?

TAKE 100 PERCENT RESPONSIBILITY

It's helpful to believe life happens *from* you, not *to* you. If you believe circumstances are beyond your control, why would you try to take action, to strive for something more? I know—you wouldn't! *However*, any belief you hold, including one around writer's block (for or against), is 100 percent within your control. Take responsibility and own that—and you'll be well on your way to writing—and *becoming the writer you've always known you could be.*

LET GO OF CERTAINTY

As humans, we crave certainty. It's probably true you have been certain you have writer's block, and your limiting beliefs have become BFFs with that certainty, leaving you without all the words.

What needs to happen is for you to become 100 percent certain you *can* write when you need or want to, so let's flip that belief around.

Example:

Prior belief: *I have writer's block.*

New belief: *When I sit down to write, the words always flow like water out of a faucet.*

This dovetails nicely with our final step:

CHANGE YOUR SELF-TALK

Your new belief can now become your daily mantra.

How's this for something cool? Positive psychology has identified that what we say when we talk to ourselves is critical to our success.

In fact, if you say something to yourself (like a new mantra), over time, one of two things will happen: you're going to do it *or* stop saying it. Yup, even if what you're saying isn't true at the moment.

I recommend taking that new belief, embracing it as your new mantra *and the new truth about you*, and saying it to yourself every single chance you get.

You can say to yourself: *I write every day.*

In fact, you can use it to your long-term advantage and reinforce that this new belief *is* the new truth about you—even while you're watching videos, eating pizza, and drinking a milkshake—while you're definitely not writing.

Commit to saying it over and over. Fifteen times is a solid number choice here, every day, and guess what? *Eventually*, you will write every day. Or you'll notice you forgot to, or stopped, saying your mantra.

What you say when you talk to yourself eventually comes to fruition. What you utter literally becomes true in your outer world.

It's a fun idea to work with—and even if you're skeptical, I hope you'll give it a try. I promise it works. And why not try it? What have you got to lose?

Have you done the exercises in this chapter? (I've got them on the next page, just in case you haven't gotten to them yet.) Then it's time for you to become the writer you've always known you could be.

CHAPTER FOUR EXERCISE

Write your old questions, then turn them into new questions.

Now, flip the script on your beliefs. Write your prior beliefs, then turn them into new beliefs.

Use your journal or the I Am a Writer! Notebook *and take as much space as you need for this (and every) exercise.*

CHAPTER FIVE

BECOME THE WRITER YOU'VE ALWAYS KNOWN YOU COULD BE

You've always known, in your heart, *I am a writer.* If not, writer's block wouldn't be on your radar. You wouldn't have picked up a book on it, or had the thought, *If I could get past this writer's block, all would be well.*

So, Mr. or Ms. I'm A. Writer, how about we put that block on ice permanently and get you into the full swing of writing? Can you become the writer you've always known you could be?

Yes!

Hopefully, you have created good questions and new empowering beliefs to take the next steps toward a life of prolific writing.

James Clear, the author of *Atomic Habits*, suggests that instead of thinking about *doing* something for an outcome, focus on *becoming* who you want to be.

You wouldn't say, "I clean houses." You'd say, "I am a housekeeper." Nor would you say, "I write legal contracts." You'd say, "I am a lawyer." It stands to reason you would benefit from this day forward from owning that you are a writer in everything you think and say. I know it would. It does!

Let's beef it up a bit, too, by making it a complex sentence.

"I am writing because I am a writer."

Forget about writer's block for a minute and say it with me.

"I am writing because I am a writer."

Note: Eventually, you won't think about writer's block at all. If you doubt this, think of something that, at one time, you couldn't take your mind off—and you haven't thought about it in years. You can do this with writer's block, too.

In fact, I challenge you to, henceforth, now and forever, when someone asks you what you do, answer with, "*I am a writer.*"

CREATE A NEW VISION

You can craft a new vision with your new questions and beliefs—one starring you as a writer—a prolific, productive, and happily writing professional writer.

Close your eyes for a few minutes and picture yourself with the end results of a project. Are you holding your book, admiring the beautiful cover, flipping through the pages, and marveling that all of those words were once simply in your mind?

Do you look at the big screen in a darkened theater, watching actors speak the words you wrote in your screenplay?

Or are you seeing your name as the byline in a newspaper or magazine—or many of them all at once?

Is your favorite musician singing the song you wrote while you sing along backstage?

Hey, you're a writer—grab a fresh legal pad or open up your laptop and *write out your new vision*. Make it positive, present tense, and as big, bright, and beautiful as you dare.

You might wonder if I'm encouraging you to write a vision solely about your writing. Yes. And no.

While you're at it, why not surround your vision of being a magnificent writer with the other elements of your life that could use a little up-leveling?

Include where you are—where you live and work. Who is with you? Where do you go for fun? Are you treating yourself to some long-desired items or activities, to cement and celebrate your success?

Take all the time you need. The only person this is for is you (and no one else ever needs to see it). You don't need anyone else's permission, and you can envision any single thing you'd like. Nothing is too grandiose or unachievable. *I'm sure of that.*

Go on; I'll wait right here. This is important.

Are you still with me? Still reading? Harboring a small pool of doubt? That this exercise might work for me, or for other people, but not for you? I understand.

You might not believe it could happen yet, and that's okay. I'm sure Jim Carrey didn't believe he would make ten million dollars for starring in a movie when he first envisioned it.

In addition to crafting your vision, you might be inspired to do something similar to what Jim did.

Back in 1985, long before he became a worldwide movie star, he was broke and depressed. Almost every night, he drove his old beat-up Toyota up into the Hollywood Hills, dreaming of becoming a wildly successful movie star. He wrote himself a check for ten million dollars for "*acting services rendered*," and gave himself three years to achieve it. He stuck that check in his wallet, where he'd look at it every time he paid for something.

Although the check remained there so long it deteriorated, Jim eventually made ten million dollars for starring in movies like *Ace Ventura: Pet Detective* and *Dumb and Dumber*. He put what remained of the check in his father's casket when he passed away. Here's a link to a brief clip if you'd like to hear him and Oprah talk about it: https://www.oprah.com/oprahs-lifeclass/what-oprah-learned-from-jim-carrey-video.

Do you need to write yourself a check? Put your vision in the form of a vision board or a screensaver on your phone or computer to remind you of your quest.

Hopefully, you used your imagination to craft *in writing* a compelling future (if you haven't, please do it now!). Along with having it in writing, being able to visualize it regularly will help it come faster and easier. You might want to read my book *Vision to Reality* for a more comprehensive process for turning your vision into your real-life reality.

But wait, there's more!

DEFINE YOUR PURPOSE

You might not be completely convinced that what you wrote could come true. That's why, in addition to having a crystal-clear vision, you need to define your purpose.

What's the difference? I'm so glad you asked.

Your vision is **what** you want.

Your purpose is **why** you want it.

Why do you want to be a writer? To earn a living? To become famous? To inspire? To entertain?

A strong *why* is integral to your success because you won't take consistent, persistent action (read: write) until you've got certainty around your why.

You might be able to compel yourself through the use of willpower to write for a few days, but sooner or later, if you don't know why writing is *that important*, you'll skip a day, then two, then who knows how many.

What do I mean by *that important*? To say yes to writing, you will have to say no to something else. Is it sleep? Fun with friends? Watching television?

Knowing your why will mean it will be easy to go to bed early, leave in the middle of a party, or write on your lunch hour. To say, "I'm on a deadline," and postpone other gratification in search of your goal on the way to fulfilling your vision.

No *why*? No *what*. It's as simple as that.

Once you know what you *really* want, it's imperative for you to determine your purpose—why you want that vision *more* than you want anything else.

Complete your vision with a purpose statement that is clear, concise, and *fires you up*. It's the fire within your vision and purpose that can and will propel you forward in your writing.

In addition to a vision and purpose that lights you up, I've got one more trick up my sleeve, and you just might love it.

GIVE YOURSELF AN ALTER EGO

Want to become your future fierce and fabulous writing self now, be the vision instantly instead of simply slogging away, waiting for the magical day when you realize you've made it?

You can do something, starting right now, that actors, athletes, politicians, and even professionals do: identify and embody an alter ego. They step into the person they know they need to be—who they know they want to and can be—to get the job done sooner rather than later.

Ryan Serhant talked about it in his book *Big Money Energy*. For his final audition for *Million Dollar Listing: New York*, he knew if producers followed him around while he was doing what realtors usually do—make phone calls and surf the web for hours on end (#boring)—he wouldn't get his life-changing casting. Little Ryan wouldn't get the job, but Big Ryan sure would. So instead of showing them his normal day-to-day reality, he decided to give them what he knew they wanted: a thrilling peek into the day of one of the top real estate agents in town. He borrowed a friend's Range Rover, told everyone he knew to call him so he would be perceived as busy and very successful, and even enrolled his trainer in putting him through an intense workout. He became "the best real estate broker in the world" that day, even though he wasn't quite there yet.

He did what you can do: craft an alter ego and then use it to help you keep fear at bay, show up differently, and write like a boss. Today!

Alter egos don't have writer's block. They don't spend hours staring into a glass of whiskey, wearing oversized sweats on the couch, or sleeping until noon. They don't dream about writing; they sit their fierce selves down, and when it's time to write, they write!

Chin up, shoulders back, music on, coffee black, *writing*.

Lest you think this is a silly idea, *many* people, of all ages and at various stages of success, have created an alter ego and gotten some pretty spectacular results. Until you can be your future self, why not entertain the idea you could be your future self now, by design and on demand?

Kids have Batman or Dora the Explorer. Beyoncé has Sasha Fierce, and Adele has Sasha Carter. Jennifer Lopez is, of course, JLo. Will Smith was the Fresh Prince. Who doesn't remember Marky Mark (Mark Wahlberg), Hannah Montana (Miley Cyrus), or Slim Shady (Eminem, a.k.a. Marshall Mathers)? Ryan Serhant, founder of SERHANT (a real estate brokerage firm based in New York City) talks about "Future Ryan." He focuses on leaning into the Ryan he wants to be in the future and encourages readers to take on the energy and persona of the person they want to be in the future—today.

You can create an alter ego that *never* has writer's block. One that is calm and centered, prolific and productive, famous or infamous, professional, successful, and prosperous.

It's entirely up to you. In case you're inspired by this idea, here's what will happen when you have an alter ego, followed by just a few steps you can use to create yours:

- You'll go after your goals with gusto.
- You'll make decisions from a place of power and self-confidence.

- You'll face challenging situations *like a boss*,
- have hard conversations (and live!), and
- speak with confidence.
- You'll set an example for those who look up to you, including you!

And those are just for starters. Who knows what will happen when you take your life and career by the horns and step into your future self? Well, you won't know if you don't give it a try, so...

Step One. Choose an alter ego name that makes you smile and, in the same moment, inspires you to dream bigger, be your best self, and go for your goals and dreams. (You could use a nickname or moniker others have given you, as long as you love it, as I have done and do.)

Step Two. Define how they talk, walk, speak, and act. How do they handle situations? *How do they write?*

Step Three. What are their beliefs, and how do they think? *How do they think about writing?*

Step Four. Have a trigger device or outfit to remind you to *be it now*. Maybe you have a suit, or a piece of jewelry, or a pair of shoes that make you feel like a million bucks when you put them on. Well, it is now a trigger to embody your alter ego.

Step Five. Use the mantra you crafted a couple of chapters ago *all the time*.

Step Six. When you start to feel like procrastinating instead of writing, self-doubt creeps in, or someone says something less than awesome to you, try this: Instead of "No, because...," say, "Yes, and..." to any opportunity (even if you don't think it's possible). (Say yes and figure out the how later!)

- Can you write? "Yes, and I can do it before I go to work."
- Are you a writer? "Yes, and I'm writing more all the time."
- Are you going to become a full-time professional writer? "Yes, and I have so many opportunities, more every day."

Guess what? This should be a fun exercise because *you are a writer*. You should have a very easy time describing your alter ego in full, living color. Amiright?

Maybe my example would be helpful.

Note: my introverted, *very* private self is shouting, "No f-ing way you're going to share this! Tamp it down, Honorée Corder! Tamp. It. Down!" Meanwhile, H-Money says, "How the heck are you going to help your readers? How are they going to know where to start if you don't give them an authentic example? F-yeah, you're sharing!"

As you may have guessed, my alter ego is "H-Money," a nickname from several of my friends and mastermind members. One of my friends' kids even calls me Auntie H-Money.

She has a strong, confident presence, is kind and funny, and doesn't take herself too seriously. But she takes her work seriously and fiercely loves those she works with. She's never met a stranger and wants to help everyone she meets. She makes positive choices (even when she doesn't want to) and isn't afraid to own her mistakes (which she makes a lot—because that's the only way to figure out how much life she can get out of this one and only life she has). She writes as easily as she breathes and has a great time doing it. And she's infinitely creative—always has tons of ideas and is able to come up with ideas that help everyone she talks to—and happily shares those ideas. She does well because she does good.

I have a few pieces of jewelry and a pair of red heels that remind me to be "H-Money." One is a necklace I wear *all the time*, and I've programmed myself to go right into H-Money Mode when I see it in the mirror or reach up and touch it. In fact, I would say that my introverted self and my alter ego are one and the same pretty much all the time. If you try this, I think you'll find that happens, too.

Now, with any luck, all of the alter ego examples I've shared, including mine, have inspired you to combine your vision and purpose statements with a magnetic alter ego that simply propels you forward at rocket speed.

Getting what boils down to your internal psychology in order is one piece of the puzzle. An important piece, no doubt, yet there are a few more aspects of leaving writer's block behind for good that still need to happen.

It's time to …

CHAPTER FIVE EXERCISE

Grab a 3x5 card and write *I am a writer* on it.

Then, grab your journal (or computer) and write your vision (start with bullet points, then expand on each one). This is *easy* because you are a writer!

Define your purpose in writing after you've completed your vision.

Crank out an alter ego that makes you smile and feel fierce and fabulous all at the same time.

"The secret of getting ahead is getting started. The secret of getting started is breaking your complex overwhelming tasks into small manageable tasks, and then starting on the first one."

—Mark Twain

CHAPTER SIX

CLEAR THE DECKS & SET THE (WRITING) STAGE

With a clear vision and purpose, plus an alter ego that simultaneously makes you smile and fills you with "let's do this!" energy, you've got the necessary *joie de vivre* to make some serious progress in your writing.

Let's seal your fate as a productive, prolific writer, while simultaneously heading off any future road (or writer's) blocks where you might not feel exactly the same amount of fabulous you do right now.

This is where "woo woo" meets "what are we actually going to *do*?" I love to marry practical practices with mystical principles. Let me say this in two ways that, with any luck, easily convey:

- As you *talk* about it, you must also *be* about it.
- As you pray, move your feet.

You won't take consistent action if you don't believe you're going to get excellent results. Conversely, I don't think one can sit around and hope desired results appear. While hope is absolutely a must-have, it is not a strategy for success—writing or otherwise.

If you've completed the previous chapters' exercises, you've laid the groundwork for some awesome productivity. This chapter is designed to help you put next-level measures in place to all but ensure your success. First, you must...

DO YOUR WORK

You've identified your new beliefs, solidified your vision, defined your purpose, and now you're ready, right? Maybe.

You need to know you can write wherever you want, whenever you want—regardless of what's going on around you.

Regardless of how hard it has ever been for you to write, please remember: your past performance or lack thereof does not predict your future. You do.

You need to—and want to—be confident that the framework you've built around yourself and your writing will hold, and you will follow through. Be certain when you say, "I'm going to write from 6:00 to 7:00 a.m., five days a week," that it's something you will stick to.

I've got a few tips for closing the gap and getting your productivity in motion once and for all.

Now, I want to make sure you've done this book's exercises. That you didn't keep reading instead of

- Penciling out a new belief or three
- Writing your vision
- Putting clarity behind your purpose
- Defining your alter ego

Because if all you've done is read straight through to this point, intending on doing the exercises later, this next part won't be as effective. I'd love to say you can use willpower to overpower writer's block—and anything else in the way of your writing. But I'd be lying, and lying is bad.

The truth is that the work is necessary for you to become the professional, prolific writer you know you can be.

Ask any professional writer, and they will tell you they have the beliefs, vision, and purpose to write. They might even have an alter ego, even if they haven't articulated that to the world. And they for darned sure have done the work. Otherwise, how on earth would they be able to write so much, and so consistently?

There may be plenty of professional writers reading this who are thinking, *I still have writer's block.* Allow me to be kindly blunt here: *you still have some work to do, too.*

I would be remiss if I didn't mention that sometimes there is work of a very personal nature that falls outside of the parameters of this book. I'm not qualified to speak to any blocks you have stemming from trauma, addiction, or other severe mental stress or strain. If you, like me, have a past filled with challenges that only a professional can help heal, I suggest you do that work, also.

While working with an effective therapist can yield incredible, life-changing results, it is difficult work. If you need it, consider this encouragement to face anything deeply held that's standing in your way. Working through your *stuff* will help eliminate writer's block and also any imposter syndrome that might ride along. It can suck (it sure did for me), and it will be worth it. And if you also need a hug—here's one for the journey.

For the next section, I'm assuming you've done your work (or are committed to doing it) and are ready for the next level. If it's time to close the loop on your ability to write *on command*, let's continue!

CLEAR THE DECKS AND SET THE STAGE

Clearing the decks is something every writer needs to do in order to put words on the page. The decks I'm referring to are

The time(s) to write. You can be all fired up and ready to write. Now you need to decide *when* you will write.

- Before you do anything else in the morning?
- On your break or lunch hour?
- In bed, before you go to sleep?

How much time do you need? I use the Pomodoro Technique (twenty-five minutes of focused writing time) in the form of two back-to-back sessions during my morning writing hour. I need an hour a day to write several books a year. You get to decide when you'll write—and your process may change over time—and once you do, put it in your calendar as an inviolate appointment.

If you'd like more guidance on finding the time to write, grab a copy of *The Nifty 15: Write Your Book in Just 15 Minutes a Day* for tons of practical tips, ideas, and strategies.

The place(s) to write. Ideally, you'll have a dedicated writing space or two.

- Will you write at your desk or kitchen table?
- At a coffee shop or library?
- In your car?

Ideally, I write at my desk in the mornings, five or six days a week. I can write anywhere. My mother-in-law's couch, on an airplane, in a coffee shop, in a hospital lobby. I've written in all of those places, and while I suggest you identify your ideal space, the goal is to write wherever you find yourself.

When you do this, the good news is you've left the door open for inspiration to strike and for you to get those words down.

The energy to write. This is big: Having the energy to write presupposes you are rested, recharged, and rejuvenated. Let's also add to this list: You're hydrated, nourished, and you've exercised (walking is exercise) and maybe even had a quick meditation.

Excellent self-care is not always easy when you're not a full-time writer (and even when you are). The truth is words flow freely from a rested mind and a healthy body. That means you need to get enough of everything you need to function as your writer's highest self *and* have enough white space to allow your creative juices to flow.

If you're not getting enough sleep, what needs to happen so you can?

- Go to bed earlier?
- Take a disco nap midday?
- Stop drinking caffeine at 2 p.m.?

If you don't have enough white space on your calendar for inspiration, what needs to happen so you do?

- Block time on your calendar for thinking time?
- Take more vacations or holidays?
- Have shorter workdays?

- Say *no* to something (what?) so you can say *yes* to yourself and your goals?
- Or, do something else?

I find writing incredibly difficult when I'm tired (or stressed). It's like pushing a huge boulder uphill in the sun on a hot August day.

In fact, it is not easy for me to write when I'm hungry, thirsty, or grouchy.

Let me throw sad in here, too, as during the writing of this book, I lost my beloved cat of a dozen years, Mr. Pickles. It's also hard to write when one is grieving. If this is you, just keep putting one foot and one word in front of the other as you can and know that the sun will rise again. (And hang in there.)

If you've got a lot of life stress, keep reading—I've got an entire section on that coming right up.

Now, I have learned what works for me, and it is every single one of those bullets. I must take excellent care of myself, including getting enough rest and managing my schedule. In order to have the brain power and time to write, it's imperative I take breaks throughout the day, rest on weekends, and take plenty of time off throughout the year. Also, since I start my day early, I plan to finish early. Save but for a few times a year (I see you, Empire Builders Mastermind members!), I do my best to *not* burn the candle at both ends.

I'm going to add one more crucial piece to the self-care equals prolific writer list: *time to do nothing*. When I say white space, that's what I mean. Space that has nothing in it. Also known as "think time," you can and might want to add blocks of time on your calendar to sit and think, allowing your creative mind to wander and, well, create.

Alternatively, white space allows you to take an hours-long nap, read for pleasure, watch old (or new) movies, or your favorite television show, go for a picnic, visit a museum, or go for a walk.

If you need a reminder that you're a human being, not a human doing; this is it.

Figuring out how to keep your batteries charged is going to help those words flow a lot faster and more often. You must fill your well of creativity from the inside and outside.

If you're not rested, hydrated, nourished, and moving your body on the regular, how can you recalibrate your schedule so you can?

You may find that any writer's block you've experienced up to this point can find its roots in trying to fit writing into the cracks of your schedule, all while there are cracks in your personal foundation.

The support to write. Your most significant relationships are going to impact your writing. Everyone needs to be enrolled in the "I'm a writer!" program.

My husband, Byron, is a night owl. He'd love it if I'd stay up (and out) late, yet he's supportive of my goals. He often jokes with me as the sun sets at 4:30 p.m. (anyone else not a fan of Daylight Savings?), "Isn't it almost time for bed?" He's not entirely off—during the summer as well as all of the other seasons, my goal is to be lights out and asleep around 9:00 or 9:30 p.m.

If he weren't supportive or was constantly encouraging me to do things not in alignment with my goals, it would be almost impossible for me to wake up before my 4:30 a.m. alarm and be writing this right now.

How do you enroll those closest to you to support your goals? *You talk to them.*

I have mine on the bathroom mirror, so they're hard to miss. Yet I've found a conversation is also in order. Try, "I'd love to tell you what I'm working on and what my goals are. In fact,

I'd love it if you helped hold me accountable and reminded me to make choices that serve my desired outcomes." My language, not yours. You're a writer, so wordsmith how you want to say it.

Sometimes it's hard enough to get ourselves to write (or do anything), so having your biggest fan standing watch with encouraging words *is awesome*.

I can almost hear some of my readers thinking, *What if my people don't understand or aren't supportive?*

I will tell you what I told one of the previous members of my mastermind: "You are a grown woman. You can do what you want to do. You can also not do what you don't want to do."

You have the freedom to say "yes" or "no" as you please.

It can be hard to stick to your guns, especially if your most intimate of relationships isn't supportive, but *you can do it*.

If someone is constantly encouraging you to do things counterproductive to your writing goals, simply say, "No, thanks." ("No." is a complete sentence, after all.) If they ask why, you can add, "That's not in alignment with my goals."

The discipline to write. Having the discipline to write can be tricky. What masquerades as writer's block could actually be our very naughty, sneaky friend, procrastination. (This friend would much rather do anything but write, especially if that anything else involves eating pizza, staying up late, and possibly drinking a cocktail.)

Meaning to write is different from scheduling time to write.

Trying to write is different from actually writing.

Scheduling time to write and then sitting down to write, only to get distracted, equals few to no words on your page.

As I am not a psychologist, only someone who has chosen to keep trying and eventually learn what works for me, I cannot speak to why exactly some have discipline and others do not.

I can, however, hypothesize from experience, and here's what I've got for you, fellow scribe:

- Discipline comes from habit.
- Habit comes from actions.
- And actions come from decisions.

When I'm asked, "How do you write so many books?" my first answer is "It's my job." I am a writer. I write, and I write books.

Underneath that discipline is my daily writing habit of taking action (writing) based on my decision to write. It might be helpful to have a peek behind my decision process, which, as you can see, ultimately results in a book like the one you're reading now.

Step One: The Decision. I decide to write a book. Rooted in that decision is *what kind of book (short or traditional), publication date (plus the commensurate schedule), ancillary offerings (Workbook? Journal? Course?), and the job of the book.*

Step Two: Action. I take action. I define my production and publication schedule, outline the book, and book dates with my team.

Step Three: Discipline. I write. Every morning, two Pomodoros, between 5:30 and 7:00 a.m., give or take, based on my day. Every weekday and some Saturdays, save holidays, vacations, and special circumstances. It's a habit. When I do it, the day is off on the right foot. When I don't, I feel a little off. I feel great on the weekends when I know my "job" is to rest, fill up my reserves, and relax.

Wrapped around my discipline is the commitment to say *no* to anything not aligned with my goals. Is it tempting to stay up and finish another episode or chapter? You bet it is! Would it probably be more fun to stay out late, get to bed late, and shift my alarm? Obviously! My inner child wants to go rogue and throw caution to the wind. She throws temper tantrums every week, at least once—when I'm at an event, and I know if I don't leave and get home to bed, I'll regret it when my alarm goes off. Or when I'm at 96 percent of a great thriller, and I could finish it in another twenty minutes ("What's twenty minutes?"), I have to close it and finish it the next day. (And I've got H-Money right there, keeping my inner child in check.)

I want to wake up rested so these words feel like they are writing themselves. I've tried it "the other way" (on the uphill side of not having enough rest), and it doesn't work.

You'll note I talked about energy before discipline, and here's why: I take many breaks—weekends, holidays, and weeks and weeks of vacation every year—and during those breaks, *I mostly do not write.* It's not on the calendar! (Yes, I still rise early, and in those hours, I am doing much more reading. It is heavenly.) So guess what? I don't really want to miss writing when it *is* on the calendar. I've got the energy and the discipline, and I am ready to go. I tell my inner child she can slow her roll; she's got a break coming up, and she can stay up all night if she wants to (turns out she doesn't).

Staying aligned with your goals, depending on what they are on any given day, will serve you over the long term. It will help you figure out what works for you so you can wrap your decisions and structure around your goals and objectives.

You and your writing deserve it!

All of that to say: What are you going to give up to write? Fun with friends? Sleep? Television? What will you say *no* to, and in the process, say *yes* to, in order to become the writer you want to be? Today might be the day to be productive so that someday you'll get to party like it's 1999. Just sayin'.

Let's get into something a little less heavy.

The tools to write. Having the right tools to write effectively can be a game changer. Whether you write by hand, on a device (phone, computer, or tablet), or you dictate, reliable tools make all the difference. What do you need to write at your best?

The good news is that you can write by hand, or on your phone or laptop. You don't need anything fancy or expensive. You can start writing today, right now, with any writing instrument, on the back of an envelope that started as junk mail. But having the right tools will accelerate your progress.

Here are a few tools to get you started:

- **A computer.** I'm partial to Macs, but I wrote my first book on a PC.
- **Microsoft Word or Google Docs.** I work in the former and from a template that is formatted to feel like I'm writing a book (it has a Title Page, Table of Contents, space for my Front and Back Matter, etc.).
- **A Bullet Journal, the Notes App, and Evernote.** These are the three places I capture my thoughts and resources for each project. Depending on what I'm doing when inspiration strikes (getting ready for the day, working out, driving, having a meeting, etc.) or when I stumble across something I want to include, I'll write it in my journal, capture it on my phone in the Notes app, or send myself a quick email to Evernote.

- **Scrivener.** This writing software allows you to write in "uninterrupted mode," and for each writing project, provides the space to write, organize your additional thoughts and resources, and move things around as desired. I don't use it (old dog, cough), but soooooo many of my writer friends do—and they swear by it!

This is pretty much it—not much is needed to be a writer, as it turns out. Figure out what you need to start writing right now. You can get other tools as time passes, and you learn more about how you work best.

THE S WORD: STRESS

The X factor in all of this is stress. Got any? Of course you do! Whether or not it's good stress, it acts as a slow leak in your productivity tires.

Stress affects our ability to be creative, either slowing our flow to a trickle or, sometimes, shutting it down entirely.

Lest you think I'm a writing machine who not only has the time, energy, support, discipline, and tools to write (not to mention other resources), obviously, I must also have zero stress—thus the reason I can be so prolific. Ha!

If only this were true.

Turns out, I have plenty of both good and not-so-good stress, just like you. Does my story matter? Should we compare notes to see who has it better or worse? My answer is a firm *no* to both—because it's all relative. Yours feels big to you—and it is. Mine feels big to me—and it is.

If it feels like you're running as fast as you can, holding it all together MacGyver style, with some duct tape and a paper clip, then you are.

This is the part where I direct you right back to my self-care advice. You can write more than you might think, *and* there will be times you'll need to throw up your hands, give yourself grace, and give it another go tomorrow.

One other thought: My writing is also my refuge. Even during those times when everything is burning all around me, it's my place to go, and it's what I do for me. Yes, it is also my job—and I love my job!

There have also been times of stress when my creative well seemed to be dry. In fact, there were a few years when I didn't publish very much at all, and I honestly thought I was "out of words" and ideas.

Once the smoke cleared, so to speak, I was back to my former "more ideas than time" self. This shift caused me to think about stress and writer's block in a different way. I pondered whether I had writer's block during those years and came to the conclusion it wasn't writer's block—it was straight-up stress! I only had so much energy to go around and needed to focus on other business at hand, and so I did.

Can you remember why you wanted to be a writer in the first place? Surely you didn't aspire to write under duress. Perhaps you've been writing short stories since you were five or found yourself to be a surprise writer as an adult (this is me), or you fell in love with writing, and maybe it is all you want to do.

I encourage you to seek out the genesis of that love, find it, and guard it ferociously. Everything in existence began when someone wrote it down. *You are a writer—and writers are magnificent.*

Find your love of writing and, if stress could be at the root of your lack of words, do what is necessary to mitigate your stress. Get the support you need. Go for a walk. Sleep longer. Meditate. Take up yoga or karate. *Write* and don't look at it like it's something you *have to do*; rather, it is something you are blessed to do. I know it will benefit you to find a new perspective even as you try new ways to find your flow again.

With any luck, this has helped you put context around your lack of writing. I truly want you to be the writer you've always wanted to be.

Now you have an understanding (a) there are decks you need to clear, and (b) started at least thinking about clearing them. What's next? Well, once you've cleared the decks, it's time to set the—*your*—stage!

Setting the stage. This is another way to say: putting systems, strategies, and yourself in place. Chefs do this before cooking; it's referred to as *mise en place*. Cookware, utensils, and food are prepped such that the cooking process goes quickly and smoothly.

With writing, clearing the decks is just the first part of an equation.

Clearing the decks + setting the stage = writing. Lots of writing!

Now you can prep for writing in a way that capitalizes on all you've done to get your butt in the chair and the words flowing. Here are a few things to help:

Put your writing situation in place. I work in my work-in-progress (WIP) document every morning, so at night, when I'm done for the day, I'll open it so that when I open my computer in the morning, it's the first thing I see.

My desk is cleared and ready the night before (sometimes this is quite a feat), and my Bullet Journal is open and prepped for the day. I eliminate distractions, and other than cups of coffee and tea, all I need is my computer, the manuscript, and some great music. Then I'm ready to write.

You'll want to figure out what you need to have in place so that when it is time to write, you are *good to go*. It will add frustration to your situation if you have the time to write and still need to get yourself organized.

Make a note to yourself—or, as I do, set an alarm—to remind you to *mise en place* in advance of your next writing session. Your future self is going to be psyched and grateful.

Gamify. My goal during my two Pomodoros is to write a total of one thousand words. I'm a fairly fast typist, so if I (a) know what I'm going to write and (b) stay focused, I can generally do that during the writing of a first draft. (Thank you, seventh-grade typing class.) I know, a thousand is a lot. Just a reminder, I've been doing this awhile, and my writing muscles are strong.

If you're early in your writing career, set a goal that feels achievable (and a tiny bit of a stretch). Can you strive for 250 words? Five hundred? If you're more advanced, have a tracker (I've included one in this book's bonuses you can download, visit HonoreeCorder.com/JustWrite to grab yours), and keep track of one or two weeks' worth of writing, one day at a time. Determine your daily average and make continuing that average your first goal. Your second goal, after a few weeks of (fairly) consistent writing, might be to bump it up by 50 or 100 words.

Here's the truth, though, sometimes I write as few as 200, and other days as many as 1,500. I gamify my word count simply by counting. Tracking your numbers is one way to hold yourself accountable. It's fun to put a positive word count on the tracker every day. I keep a tracker as the last page of my manuscript, and at the close of every day's writing session, I make a note of my word count. It keeps me focused—and it keeps me honest with myself.

Following are a few questions I ask myself. You might want to use them or craft a few of your own.

- Am I writing every day I am scheduled to write?
- How many words am I writing?
- How many Pomodoros am I doing—am I sticking with two or just squeezing in one or not even quite one?

If a tracker sounds terrible, make a note in your planner or Bullet Journal on each day's date how many words you wrote. Print out a monthly calendar and write the number of words you've written on each day as you go.

Oh, by the way! This is *not* an opportunity for you to beat yourself up when you don't write, can't write, or miss a day or several in a row. The root of gamify is games, and games are fun. Keep it fun, friend, and your inner child will want to play (read: write). Make yourself feel bad or wrong for any part of this, and we're back on the (writer's) block in a jiffy.

Prime the pump. Whether you handwrite in your journal or type a silly phrase (example: *just keep writing, just keep writing, just keep writing*) over and over until project-specific words start to flow, sometimes it is helpful to write anything besides the project at hand in order for the words to flow.

You can also prime the pump by reading what others have written on your topic. I read a bunch of articles on writer's block, found quotes by writers who believe in it (and those who don't), and even another book of a similar title.

The Artist's Way by Julia Cameron is a popular book among creatives, encouraging writers to write, in longhand, three pages a day, every day, stream of consciousness.

When the book was first released, I got a copy and faithfully wrote my three pages a day for a long time. *Long* before I considered myself a creative, I was into personal development, and I found the book in that section at the bookstore. I wonder now if it was the impetus behind my ability to easily write today. It might possibly be why my writing muscles are developed. Morning pages might help you develop yours as well.

Set a deadline and a goal. There's nothing like a deadline to add fuel to your fire. Professional writers have deadlines—internal or external—and they meet those deadlines. It's just what they do.

If you're still getting your bearings, set a deadline and right alongside it, a word count goal. Depending on your previous experience, you might set a goal to write an average of 250 words over the next thirty days—or a goal of 1,000 words a day, three days a week, over the next six months until you've finished the first draft of your manuscript.

Are you a songwriter? Write for the wastebasket. Write song after song and tell yourself you're going to throw the "bad" ones in the trash (but don't do this—save those songs—you may find you need a lyric or line in the future).

Maybe you're a poet. Same idea. *Just write.* Write and keep writing *until.*

Until when? Just until. Read: never stop.

In the next chapter, I will share one of the most effective ways to eliminate writer's block and stay in the flow of writing. When you're ready, turn the page to do your chapter exercises, and then continue reading.

CHAPTER SIX EXERCISE

It's time to set your stage!

When will you write?

Where will you write?

How will you ensure you have the energy to write?

Who needs to support you, and how will you help them to do that?

What decisions, habits, and actions do you need to engage the discipline to write?

What are the tools you need to write?

What stress do you need to manage or mitigate?

> "The best way is always to stop when you are going good and when you know what will happen next. If you do that every day … you will never be stuck. Always stop while you are going good and don't think about it or worry about it until you start to write the next day. That way, your subconscious will work on it all the time. But if you think about it consciously or worry about it you will kill it and your brain will be tired before you start."
>
> —Ernest Hemingway

CHAPTER SEVEN

SURROUND YOURSELF WITH OTHER WRITERS

The secret sauce of success in any area of discipline is *community*. As writers, we work mostly in solitude (and it can get quite lonely!), so I believe the need for—and the benefits of—a writing community cannot be underestimated. My discovery of other writers was life-changing.

Creating a personal community of other writers is your ticket to ride! Many writers report being introverts (those who prefer to be alone, as well as those who recharge alone). Having friends and confidants who speak the same language, have the same goals, aspirations, *and* challenges, and can provide encouragement, is more beneficial that I can possibly stress in one paragraph.

This chapter will help you understand the power and benefits of surrounding yourself with other writers at all levels, and then help you find and connect with them. Yes, fellow writers get a whole chapter in a book about writer's block because, all things being equal (and if none of the other challenges mentioned in this book exist for you), *not* having relationships with other writers can mean the difference between writing fluidly and not writing at all.

In your writing career, there will be writers ahead of you on the journey. These are your mentors (stated or unstated). I've had mentors who have never heard of me and mentors I've had the privilege of getting to know. You get to decide who your writing role models and mentors are and use their success as a beacon.

You'll also want friends who are writers—lots of them, and for a multitude of reasons. Building your bench of friends who are writers will inject much-needed levity, companionship, and ideas, and the resulting creativity is just the best!

The fun part of developing writer friends is that sometimes they start out as mentors (you read their books, love them, and learn from them), and then one day, you get to befriend them. *So cool.* Let's start with mentors.

MENTORS

Trying to figure things out on your own can waste time, money, and energy, and raise your stress level, and the by-product of this is (you guessed it!) *no writing*.

You can learn from a mentor by observing what they do from afar. Or you can connect with them, and they could provide personal insight and wisdom. Either way, what they have is a positive impact on your writing because you get to learn from them.

Before I mention some of my mentors and friends, I want to note I am not "name-dropping" (that would be gauche). With any luck, I'm inspiring you to reach out to other writers you admire because goodness loves goodness, and iron sharpens iron. What does *that* mean? It means that successful authors want to know other successful authors—and yes, sometimes *before* they are successful! Everyone has a first article, poem, song, or book. And in everyone's origin story, there is someone who reached down and pulled them up, gave them a shot, or made a life-changing introduction.

In my writing life, I've had so many mentors, but here are stories of just two that made a positive, life-changing impact:

One of my mentors is Jeffrey Gitomer. He interviewed me on the *Sell or Die* podcast for the launch of *The Bestselling Book Formula*.

On the show, I told the story of what he said to me when I handed him the first version of my very first book almost two decades ago (which was absolutely horrible, very bad, and no copies remain that will see the light of day):

I was so proud to hand him my book! I had quoted him in the book before I was introduced by a mutual friend. I had been reading the column he wrote for the local business journal for years and was a huge fan. So, of course, I was over the moon to have the opportunity to not only meet him but show him where I quoted him. In anticipation, I handed him the book, and he read it for about a minute (which I think might have been one of the longest minutes in the history of minutes).

Then he said, "You're a good writer, Honorée." (Insert premature hair flip.) "But this book is shit." Oh, dear.

He wasn't wrong—I had made every amateur mistake, and he did me a favor by telling me so. His style is very direct, and I did something others might not do—I chose to hear what he said, "This is shit," instead of interpreting it as "You are shit." I took his advice, gave it a *much* better title, hired an editor, proofreader, and graphic designer, and produced a professionally published book. The rest, as they say, is history.

Oh, did you think I was going to share that first book's original title so you could look it up and see how bad it was? Nope. I. Am. Not. Suffice it to say it shall remain nameless. LOL

Let me share my second story instead. I met Deborah Coonts, author of *Wanna Get Lucky?* (and now many other books), at a networking event for attorneys. An attorney-client had invited me; Deborah was a former-attorney-turned-novelist who was the featured speaker. I admired her instantly. With her charming sense of humor, kind demeanor, and a great book, she was someone I looked up to. She was highly educated, accomplished, and traditionally published—all the things I was *not*. Over time, we developed a friendship that has stood for almost two decades. It was impactful when she told me *I* was a real writer and should keep writing! Her words played in my head when I wondered whether I was or could be a "real author."

I want to encourage you to reach out to successful writers you admire because you never know—you could be friends!

Writers, especially successful writers, are busy creatures. There's always a lot to do—write, publish, market, repeat. Do your part—see the "Making Writer Friends" section later in this chapter—so they will see the value in connecting with you.

But first, why make the effort? I can almost hear you saying, "I don't have time to make friends!" or, "Adults don't want new friends." Stay with me on this; I promise it will be worth it a decade from now—and probably much sooner. Let me explain.

FRIENDS

Spending time identifying other writers you'd like to get to know and then putting in the time to develop a real friendship can be beneficial on multiple levels.

First, you'll have people to celebrate your wins. You've sent your first finished manuscript to an editor? Published an article or book? Did you get an agent or book deal?

Your writer friends will be right there, thrilled by your success.

But what about my spouse, partner, or BFF? Now we all have an interest or hobby the significant others in our lives don't find as mesmerizing. They will listen patiently when we "go on and on." That's one of their roles. You do the same for them, right?

But your writer buddies are thrilled to wax on for hours—or days—about word choices, the challenges writers face, which chapter goes first, is it okay to kill off a beloved character in Chapter Three, whether to publish wide or remain faithful to the 'Zon, to get an agent and a traditional deal or self-publish. The list does go on.

Second, the world runs on relationships. Am I the best writer in the world? Heck no. Do I have the biggest platform or the widest reach? Again, *nope.* I am genuinely interested in creating long-standing and valuable relationships (and I do not have an agenda other than to have a friend and be a friend). I simply want to make great friends I can hang out with on the journey, celebrate and encourage, and vice versa.

Writer friends can lift you up, make you feel great when you don't, and celebrate your wins when you have them. They want you to succeed and are there every step of the way. They also need to write (more), and turnabout is fair play—just as they're helping you, the reverse is true.

As Craig Martelle, prolific writer, and author encourager, says, "A rising tide lifts all boats."

Case in point: Dale Smith Thomas, who is a speaker and author of the delightful *Good Morning Gorgeous: Discovering Your Gorgeousness from the Inside Out,* is also a former beauty queen. We became fast friends after another mutual friend, ghostwriter Alice Sullivan, introduced us.

That beauty queen part (Mrs. Tennessee 1990) yielded an interesting story. She met a make-up artist at a pageant and loved what he told her:

"Girl, I love your hair! I hope you win!"

The thing is, your fellow scribes understand your challenges and what you're trying to do. They are there to, in essence, say to you, "I love your writing! I hope you write, publish, and win!"

In addition to cheering you on, they will introduce you to other incredible people, host a dinner party in honor of your twenty-fifth book, and promote your books or other writings to their networks.

As I write this, I'm in the midst of a book launch. Even as I check book sales, ranking, reviews, and ratings, I'm keeping tabs on a writer friend's recent release. Why? *Because I love her book, and I want her to win.*

MAKING WRITER FRIENDS

Making friends as adults could be a book in its own right. Being a relatively new Tennessean, I moved here at almost fifty. Although I'd heard many times, "Moving to a new place? Wow, it's hard to make friends at your age!" I chose not to embrace that idea.

I understand a few things about human behavior, and here are three of them:

- If you want to have a friend, you have to be a friend. Yes, we learned this in kindergarten.
- People always have room for a new person in their life if that person is authentic and adds value. (Bonus points if you're fun!)
- Not all friendships are instantaneous (most are not!); they take time and effort.

WANT A FRIEND? BE A FRIEND.

I have many friends who started out as someone I simply admired from afar.

I'd seen them speak at a conference and had been blown away. One such friend is Beth Walker, author of *Never Pay Retail for College*. We worked together in a coaching capacity and eventually collaborated on a book (*The Successful Single Mom Gets an Education*), and we have remained friends for almost two decades. We've recently reconnected on a deeper level, and we're going to get to work together even more in the future.

In more than a few cases, I've read their books with highlighters over and over. There are many of these folks in my life, and you can experience this in your life, too.

Now you might be wondering, *but how did you become their friend?*

Great question! You are so smart!

CONNECTING WITH MENTORS

You might think contacting writers you admire, who are further along the path than you are, would be too difficult, bordering on impossible. The truth is the opposite. I've found on multiple occasions it was simple to make contact, plus those who responded were mostly open and kind.

I did what I suggest you do: send them a note and tell them you loved their book, poem, film, whatever. The note could be in the mail or via social media.

Want to speed up your connections? Here's a quick three-step process.

- **First connection.** Follow them on the web. Figure out where they post the most often and like and comment on their posts. You can subscribe to their YouTube channel, connect with them on LinkedIn, and attend their summits or webinars.
- **Second connection.** Read their bio—chances are, there's a link to their website. There, you can sign up to be on their email list.
- **Third connection.** If they have a book, get the book. Read it. Make notes, and highlight your favorite quotes and passages. Write a meaningful review and post about it on your social media (be sure to tag them); maybe send them an email.

Even the most successful writers are paying attention to their online engagement (even if they have hired a team to handle it). They will likely recognize your name if they see it enough times. In a delightful way, you will become familiar to the person you want to connect with.

It could take months or years, but honestly, aren't you in it for the long term? Aren't you a professional intending to be around for the long haul and eventually become a known force in your space? Yeah, I thought so. Then you'll want to know and be known by all the other cool kids in that space.

Your first three steps are just that—your first three steps of many. In fact, the number of steps or touches in a relationship is incalculable. And who wants to keep track anyway? You're friends and friends connect and reconnect as needed.

THERE'S ONE MORE OPPORTUNITY …

Do you wonder whether I've spent an inordinate amount of time online, spending my days stalking people intentionally on the internet and making these connections? Umm, no, that would be weird.

Yo, don't make this weird!

I've followed those three steps for dozens of fellow writers over the years so that by the time

I connected with them face-to-face, they knew my name.

Now, I have the advantage of having a unique name, one that made my formative years interesting and somewhat brutal. It has worked to my advantage as an adult. However, you don't need a notable name to be memorable.

You do need to be friendly, positive, and consistent so that when you meet your intended friend in person, they already feel like they know you a little (or a lot). They'll feel comfortable because you've shown yourself to be a "friendly," and more than likely, they'll be thrilled to meet you.

GET TO IT, HONORÉE. WHERE DO I MEET THEM?

Okay, settle down. I was making a point. There are two ways I have met just about everyone: at a conference, or by an introduction that led to coffee, lunch, or Zoom meeting.

CONFERENCES

Writers write solo, but they love to attend conferences. Are there conferences, you ask? Are there conferences?!? Yes, by the dozens. Hundreds!

Listening to a podcast was where I discovered my first indie writer's conference. Meeting my first writer friends at that conference changed my life, and a lot of my connections have led back to it.

Here are just a few writer's conferences:

- NINC (Novelists, Inc.) *for fiction authors*
- 20Booksto50K *for nonfiction and fiction indie (self-published) authors*
- ThrillerFest *for thriller, mystery, and suspense writers*
- ALA (American Library Association) *for authors and librarians to connect*
- Killer Nashville *for thriller, mystery, and suspense writers*

There are so many! Just search for "writers' conferences," and you'll find what you're looking for—in fact, I took a quick break to do just that and found there are *hundreds*.

Conferences hold several types of possible, valuable connections:

1. **The organizers.** The folks who put on the show are the ones to know! Thank them for all of their hard work (events take a lot of time and money to do well), and even

volunteer to help if you are able. Follow up with a note of thanks afterward as a terrific way to make yourself memorable.

2. The speakers. Chances are that the speakers are authors and among those you need to know. Attend their sessions, follow them on social media, and chat with them after their presentation.

3. The sponsors. These are the folks who put their capital behind an event. They will be people you should know, and they will also be connected to others you should know.

4. The attendees. You'll find your peers and those who are miles ahead of you—all looking to connect with others. There are dozens of books and other resources on how to network at events—study networking like it is your job (because, well, it is!).

My hack for meeting the best people at conferences is to just hang out in the lobby. I generally skip the speaker's sessions, unless it is on a topic I want to learn more about or is given by someone I want to know better (or a writer friend I want to support). It is well known that the best relationships start in the lobby or the hallway. I park myself in the lobby and leave myself open to organic conversations. Lots of my writer friendships have started that way.

You don't need to wait for a conference to connect with other writers. They are everywhere! You can find writers anywhere people gather: association meetings, community service organization meetings (Rotary, Lions Club), and through volunteering. You just never know when you'll cross paths with an awesome author.

BY INTRODUCTION

You can get connected to other fabulous people through current connections. How do you know who knows who? With a little detective work, it's easy.

On LinkedIn, you can look someone up and see who you have in common. In the next section, I'll share a quick process for connecting. If you have a few or many connections in common, chances are you should be directly connected.

Recently I discovered a pretty cool author—we'd released books at the same time. I reached out to a mutual contact, one I know very well, and asked her how well she knew him. She knew him very well, pondered why she hadn't thought to connect us, and then connected us. We exchanged emails and got together over Zoom for a quick chat. Turns out we do similar things and can refer business to each other, are attending the same conference later in the year, and really hit it off.

A warm introduction can hasten a connection. The person who introduces you vouches for you, giving the person you want to meet a reason to like you ahead of your meeting.

You can still connect to just about anyone, even if you don't have any mutual connections. All you need to do is *reach out and say hello*.

REACHING OUT AND SAYING HELLO

When I come across someone fantastic, I immediately look them up online. What's happening on their website? Can I subscribe to their newsletter? Do they have a LinkedIn profile? Any other social media presence? A podcast? I look to see what they've posted and how recently they've been active.

If it seems like we would benefit from knowing each other, I get in touch. Without someone of note in common, I take the initiative to see whether they are as cool as I think they are, and I reach out.

Sometimes I email them, and other times send a message through one of their social media platforms. And then I wait. I know they'll need time to (a) see my message, (b) check me out and see whether I'm someone they want to meet, and (c) send their response.

Here's what generally happens:

1. They are awesome! They'll respond to my message, and we look for a time to schedule some kind of chat. If they are close enough geographically or will be, I like to get together in person. (While Zoom is wonderful, there's nothing like being in someone's presence to give you a real sense of them.)

2. They are neutral or lukewarm. When I send a short message and get a "Thank you!" in return, I understand they need more time, or they aren't as gung ho as I am to connect. If I really want to connect with them over the long term (and I do, based on my research), I will make it a point to continue to be on their radar from time to time until they've gotten to a place where they are more comfortable to get more connected.

3. They are defensive and (sometimes) rude. Some people feel like others in their same space are a threat, that we're playing a zero-sum game as professionals. They immediately default to "Why do you want to talk?" which I read as "What do you want?" Well, I just want to know fantastic people. Those who react in this way I put in the "maybe someday" category and hope we cross paths and connect, but I'm not holding my breath. (If this happens, don't take it personally.)

People are busy. I am busy! *I am on a deadline!* (If you know, you know.) Sometimes I send short answers, don't have time to dive deeper, or fail to see the value in creating a connection with someone who reaches out to me.

You'll find that most of your connection requests will bear fruit *over time*. Connections and friendships take time to develop, and as long as you're long-term focused, you'll look up a few years from now and marvel at the relationships that have developed.

Keep an eye out for people who live on the level of excellence. When you discover them, do some due diligence and reconnaissance until you figure out whether they are someone you'd like to know, and if they are, begin that process.

It is so worth it!

A NOTE ON NICE

Always be nice.

I can't count on two hands the number of times people have told me later, sometimes years later, about our initial encounter. The one thing they say is, "You were so nice."

While this isn't about me, my intention can help you set your intention: to always be nice to everyone you encounter. Not only because everyone is dealing with something and being nice is welcome, and not because someday the person you meet could do something for you. It is because being nice is like planting beautiful flowers. *Plant beautiful flowers.*

Plus, in the future, how you've treated someone will come back to you. The folks I've been nice to throughout the years have gone from being random encounters to casual acquaintances to (sometimes) close friends.

If being nice doesn't resonate with you, and you think it might be a waste of time, consider this:

You see the same people on the way down that you see on the way up.

Eliminating writer's block could mean soon you'll be at the top of your game. However, your mega-star status as the screenwriter of today's hottest movie or the book on *The New York Times* Bestseller List twenty weeks in a row will someday be yesterday's news. You might be tempted to believe your own press, to allow your external success to provide a false assurance that you will always be the hottest thing coming and going.

You will not.

Today's success is yesterday's news and a decade from now, perhaps entirely forgotten. And while this book is not about the cycles of life, I firmly believe that being nice will set the stage for greater success and fulfillment over time—because your network is your net wealth. Personal or professional—it doesn't matter. You need friends when you're on top of the world, and you need them when things aren't as bright as you'd like them to be.

When you're successful, it is easy to make friends, and have friends who surround you and want to be with you. When you're face down in a puddle of snot and tears and life is kicking you in the face, it is your true friends (and family) that will hold you up. Be a jerk, and you'll have a harder time working your way through your challenges, including writer's block. #justsayin'

COMMUNITY IS THE ANSWER

I started this chapter by suggesting you focus on building a community of writers around you. Your writing community, consisting of mentors and friends, can make your writing life easier, more productive, and enjoyable.

Seek wonderful, positive people you can surround yourself with, and watch the words flow from your fingertips like magic.

CHAPTER SEVEN EXERCISE

Making Friends

Identify three ways you can create a community of writer friends.

Meeting Mentors

Who are a few writers you admire and you'd love to eventually connect with on a deeper level?

Taking Action!

No friends will be made if this is just an idea you fail to act upon. So ... what will you do to create friends and connect with mentors?

CHAPTER EIGHT

LET THOSE WORDS FLOW, NOW AND FOREVER

Wow, is it Chapter Eight already? It is! You know why? *I don't have writer's block.*

You know what else? I don't want you to have it ever again, either!

You have to know, I mean, I *for sure* want you to know, I didn't write this book without a lot of thought.

I'm positive this book has raised a few eyebrows and the blood pressure of some readers.

I wrote on this topic knowing I might really upset a few people. Even my original poll on LinkedIn, "Do you believe in writer's block?" got a few snarky comments.

It isn't unusual for a contrarian position to put some people on the defensive. And although I write to help or encourage you to think, I'm uninclined to offend.

I read books and articles on writer's block. I spent many hours talking with my writer friends about their thoughts, beliefs, experiences, and attitudes about writer's block. I've reflected on why I may have moments or periods of time when the words trickle rather than flow.

It wouldn't make sense for me to just make the arbitrary statement, *there's no such thing as writer's block.*

In my nonscientific way, I came to a few conclusions backed by almost two decades of professional writing experience. Please allow my words to prime the pump of your words, by keeping these ideas handy:

Writing is like building a muscle. The more you write, the more you'll write.

As you sit down at your writing time, every day or every few days, you will write some words.

They might not be the best words, the right words, or even words you'll end up using in the end. Yet when you just put some words on the page or screen, you'll find there are others waiting to flow right behind them.

The more you write, the more you'll write, and the easier writing will become.

When I first started going to the gym in my early twenties, my trainer handed me seven-pound weights to do lateral raises. I remember thinking (and probably saying), "Seven pounds? That's way too heavy!" But it wasn't long before I had graduated from seven pounds to eight and eventually tens and twelves.

I remember breaking the six-minute mile goal I'd had for a while and my coach suggesting I could run a sub-five-minute mile. *Wow, that's fast!* I thought. It was—and I did it. *Eventually.* It took years of focused, determined training to get there.

How did I do it? I set the goal and put the work in every day until it happened.

It wasn't easy the day I did it, but it was *easier*. It required work. Sacrifice. Sweat. Seriously positive self-talk. But I did it.

Jim Rohn said, "Don't wish it was easier, wish you were better."

Don't wish writing was easier. Write until it *is* easier.

Putting in your daily word count won't always be easy. Yet it will become easier and then easy when you commit and take action despite the odds and regardless of what's happening in your world. One hundred percent commitment provides the space to make things happen.

If writing one thousand words a day feels too hard, try *training* your writing muscles with incremental increases in your word target goals:

- Every day for the next thirty days, write fifty words a day.
- For the next thirty days, write one hundred words a day.
- Double your word count for the next five months, and you'll easily write eight hundred words during your writing time.
- In the sixth month, you get to decide whether you want to shoot for doubling your word count again, or just bump it up another two hundred words to one thousand.

For any goal that feels *huge*, reduce it to the ridiculous. If running a marathon is that giant goal, start by walking fast from your front door to the mailbox. Do that for a few days, and watch how much easier it becomes as you put in the time and effort.

I write every one of my books one short writing session after another, day after day, until they are finished.

In addition to your alter ego, complete with a trigger device, what else helps you to "turn on?"

Getting "in the mood" to write is what amateurs think they need to do. Most pros will tell you that when it's time to write, they write. *However.*

Knowing how to turn your writing switch to the "on" position can markedly help. There are a few helpful action triggers I've put in place:

- **Coffee, tea, and water.** I set up my coffee and teapot every night. The next morning, I fill a water bottle and two coffee mugs and carry them all to my office (I mean, hydration is crucial, right?). Drinking a warm beverage, regardless of the time of year, goes hand-in-hand with writing.

- **Getting dressed.** Most mornings, my workout follows my writing session, so along with setting up my morning beverages, I get my morning workout and work clothes ready. Even if you work from home and no one will see you, won't *you* see you? Don't you feel better when you've put some effort into your appearance? You'll most likely find getting dressed in something other than pajamas (yes, yoga pants count) will set the stage for some great writing. Putting your best foot forward is a success secret that fits with successful writers. Plus, being prepared for anything can positively affect your writing in ways you might not imagine as you read this.

- **Music.** Writing to a soundtrack can break the seal and encourage the words. I have written almost all of my words to music, and lots of my writer friends confirm the same. You can curate a list on a music app, play an inspiring album on repeat, or put your old-fashioned radio on your favorite local station. Just as music can make a workout more fun, it can add some sparkle to your writing sessions.

- **Reading.** I *love* to read. It's a toss-up which one I love more: reading or writing. Before I ever write a single word in the morning, I read. Putting the words in helps them to come out. It's widely believed that the more writers read, the better they become. Read everything you can—regardless of whether it is in your intended genre. Great writing will inspire you to write, and that's the whole point.

- **Move!** Speaking of exercise, and understanding that the antidote to congestion is circulation, moving your body can start the flow of your words. More writers than I can count have shared that a well-timed walk helps them to write easier and unblocks their writing (and other channels of creativity) when needed.

I exercise daily, and it makes me feel good. When I feel good, I feel like writing; I enjoy it more and more often. My way isn't *the* way, yet perhaps if you're not feeling like writing and the words won't come, doing something physical to get your blood flowing will have the same results in your writing. I encourage you to find a physical activity you can rely on. If I don't feel like writing, and nothing else has gotten me in the mood, I'll clean off a shelf or tackle a messy drawer. Since cleaning isn't my favorite, as soon as my energy has shifted, I get back to writing as quickly as I can.

- **Observe Periods of Quiet.** Schedule think time, white space on your calendar and in your mind. You'll be amazed at the ideas that come when you step away from doing and just start being. I'm a huge fan of meditation, as well as periods of think time. Meditation is to your mind what rebooting is to your computer. There are apps (Calm, Headspace) and tons of other resources (YouTube videos, podcasts, and books) that provide many different practices and options. There's no right or wrong way to meditate, not too short or too long, although there's a quote about this:

"You should sit in meditation for twenty minutes every day—unless you're too busy; then you should sit for an hour." –Dr. Sukhraj Dhillon.

I discovered meditation more than thirty years ago and do at least one fifteen-minute meditation every day, most days twice. Rebooting my mental computer opens up my creative channels, and my consistent practice means I don't experience gaps in my creativity. I consider it one of my secret weapons for always being able to write on command. In addition to these daily periods of meditation, at least once a day, I grab my journal and go out on my front porch to simply sit. I set my phone aside and listen to the birds, the rain, *the sound of silence*. It is in the gap that stress leaves and ideas come.

- **Sleep is a success strategy.** When you're tired, especially if getting enough sleep is elusive, you won't feel like writing, and most likely, the words will not come. Strive for the best amount of rest to get you through your days and allow you to get in your writing. Do yourself a favor and power down at the hour you know will serve your writing, and schedule in a quick power nap during your lunch hour or mid-afternoon so you can get those words in.

With some focus, experimentation, and a sprinkle of luck, you'll be writing in no time! And when you do, you will want to pay close attention to what works the best, and eventually, you'll know your personal writer's code (which will come in handy during future times when your words are more drip and less downpour).

YOUR PERSONAL WRITER'S CODE

Keep this question in mind: When my words *are* flowing, what preceded the steady stream?

In almost every situation in life, when there is a problem, it is caused by congestion. Illness reminds us to break up the congestion in our chest. Clutter reminds us to clean up the congestion in our closets, drawers, and on our surfaces.

Writer's block is another term for congestion. When your words are flowing, let them flow! Once they finally stop, take a few minutes to identify what preceded your writing. Did you

- Get a good night's rest?
- Watch an inspiring movie?
- Go for a walk in the woods or do a workout?
- Spend time with a writer friend?
- Journal?
- Read a book that encouraged you to crack your own writer's code?
- Were you listening to great music?
- Go for a drive to clear your head and find yourself keys on keyboard?

Write it all down. This will be your "Action Signals List" to refer to in the future.

You will know what works in almost every situation to get yourself to "go" when you want to "stay put."

Your job here is to play with what works until you crack your personal writer's code. When you do, you'll be able to do it anytime you want or need to.

When you're stuck, use your Action Signals List as a cheat sheet. Write it in your journal, post it on the fridge, or get the *I Am a Writer! Notebook* and write it there.

Know that your focus and determination, as well as paying attention to what works *for you* (and what doesn't) while continuing to put one word next to the other, is going to be what creates your breakthrough.

You will have times of easy writing, and perhaps times when it isn't so easy. But *when* you keep sitting down to write, over time, you'll notice that what once was a block is now a memory.

You'll write and write and write. It won't just be something you do; *it will become who you are.*

Work with it, but better than that, play with it. There are so many people who would love to write, and you, you have that gift. *You are a writer.*

EXPONENTIALLY MULTIPLY YOUR WORDS

It bears repeating: *the more you write, the more you'll write.*

Once you've experimented with doubling your word count over a period of time and built your writing muscles, you'll be ready to jump to the next level.

What's the next level, you ask? Writing more, writing better, and writing faster. When you're feeling even the least bit confident, here are three ways to get more words than you've ever gotten before:

- **Raise your heart rate.** Do yoga, ten jumping jacks, twenty-five push-ups, or jog in place right before you write. (Yes, I'm serious.) Increasing your heart rate (*hello, circulation!*) will get your juices—and your words—flowing.

- **Mise en place.** Prep your space long before or right before. I straighten my desk before I leave my office for the day, so it is ready for the morning. I don't need to spend any time prepping my space for the day; I'm ready to write the second I sit down. Also, prepare *for* your writing by jotting down some notes, creating a quick outline, or planning your beats.

- **Learn to type faster.** Maybe what's blocked isn't the words. Perhaps you're still thinking faster than you're inking. Spend some time increasing your typing speed (try TypingTest.com).

- **Make corrections later and use placeholders.** You'll want to change things up but leave that for your first review. When you don't know what to say, type WORD and keep typing. Come back later to correct what you've written, or hang out on Thesaurus.com to discover just the right word.

- **Use DND—do not disturb.** If you're left undisturbed and can remain undistracted, you'll be able to write more than you ever thought possible. I use the DND function on my phone, iPad, and laptop, so unless something is *literally on fire* (and it never is), whatever is happening in the world will wait until I'm finished.

- **SPRINT!** The mother tip of all tips is to write like it's your job (isn't it?) and your pants are *on fire* (but, *whew*, they aren't). Set a timer and write as many words as you can until the timer goes off. Even if you write over and over, *When is the timer going off? When is the timer going off?* you'll be able to build your writing muscles faster. You can try an eight-minute sprint, a Pomodoro twenty-five-minute sprint, or write as much as you can in an hour. You can even join writing sprints on YouTube (search for "Live Writing Sprints").

- **Set the mood, start the music, start your timer.** Light a candle, put in your AirPods, press play, and *write*.

Any or all of these will eventually become your writing action signals. Once you do them consistently, over time, you'll find they spark the writing behavior you've cultivated—one of writing!

Finally, remember this:

YOU GET TO BE A WRITER

One last reminder might be the most helpful of all—writing is a privilege. You don't have to write—you get to write!

You get to, and you can! It's pretty cool when you think about it.

My sincere intention for this book is to eliminate writer's block in you and in our world. To have every writer sit down and write all they want, whenever they want, wherever they want.

As the author, the coolest outcome for me would be to receive an email from you, the reader, that says, "I used to have writer's block, but now it's a thing of the past. Now, when I sit down to write, the words flow easily from my fingertips like water from a faucet."

When this is you, please send me that email: Honoree@HonoreeCorder.com. I'll be right here on my computer, waiting to celebrate for you.

There's one more exercise for you to do. It's waiting on the next page.

From one writer to another, I wish you easy writing, effortless words, and prolific publishing.

CHAPTER EIGHT EXERCISE

Train to be a Writer

What are the ways you can increase your writing skills and speed?

How can you flip your writing switch to "on?"

What is your Personal Writer's Code?

Make your Action Signals List.

Exponentially Multiply Your Words

How can you write more, write better, write faster?

AUTHOR'S NOTES

Thank you for reading this book! I hope it exceeded your expectations and you're encouraged to become the writer you've always wanted to be.

I didn't announce this book's content as I sometimes have done in the past. I told very few people I was writing it, in fact. But during the writing, I was especially tuned in to what people said about my writing and about their own.

I did a poll on LinkedIn: *Do you believe in writer's block?* Eighty-four percent of the nineteen respondents said yes, 11 percent said no, and 5 percent said, "It's situational." One guy said,

"Who has the right to say that someone else isn't blocked? Those who deny its existence must not know what it's like to feel blocked. Lucky for them."

Facebook yielded interesting responses to my question: *Writer friends, how do you break through writer's block (or avoid it altogether)?* I changed my approach with this question and was surprised by the answers:

- "By making peace with it just being part of the process. Writer's block means I'm no longer excited for some reason. When I find that reason, I'm flying."
- "By focusing on the process and remembering the reason I want to write. Since every creative work (at least of mine) starts out mediocre, I need to make peace with being average and hope that, by continuing, something above average will one day happen."
- "ChatGPT."
- "Play in the garden, take a walk, switch projects, or quit for the day and come back to it tomorrow."
- "I think my favorite approach is to shoot for B-level writing. Sometimes we get blocked

because we're trying to make it perfect. If you resign yourself to getting a draft done quickly and making it B-quality, then editing later, it can help a lot."

- "I try to prep/outline the night before for whatever I need to write. Sometimes I just write whatever until something good shows up. And other times, I take a walk."

- "The writer's block excuse is just another distraction, like cleaning your desk or vacuuming your office when you know you should be writing. I think when you're faced with the myth of writer's block, you can always write a few paragraphs about writer's block and why you think it's bogus."

- "I use a tip from one of your books: to have a writing mantra. Every day, before I sit down to write, I recite this mantra, 'Whenever I put my fingers on the keyboard, wonderful writing flows onto the page.' It's not yet failed me. The writing may not be that wonderful, but I'm never left staring at a blank page."

I *love* that none of these answers is, "I give in and give up. I stop writing. Writer's block – 1, me – 0."

Now you: Writer – 1, Writer's Block – 0.

Happy writing!

Honorée Corder

July 2023

PLEASE REVIEW THIS BOOK

If you've enjoyed this book, would you kindly take two minutes and leave a review where you bought it (and maybe even on Goodreads.com)? I'd be eternally grateful! Thank you!

GRATITUDE

Byron, you'll probably never read this, but if you do, you already know how much I adore you. Thank you!

Renee, you're nothing short of a miracle.

To my mom, I love you.

To the team that made this book possible, I appreciate you more than words can say! Karen, you're my friend and editor, in that order. You're the best, cookie! Catherine, you're a ninja who doesn't miss *anything*. Amazing! Dino & Robert— your design work is next-level! Thanks, as always, for everything!

WHO IS HONORÉE CORDER?

Honorée Corder is a prolific author with more than fifty books (including *You Must Write a Book* and *Write Your First Nonfiction Book*) with over four and a half million sold worldwide. She's an empire builder with more than a dozen six- and seven-figure income streams and the host of the Empire Builders Mastermind, plus she's a TEDx speaker. Honorée passionately mentors aspiring empire builders, coaching them to write, publish and monetize their books, create a platform, and develop multiple streams of income.

Find out more at <u>HonoreeCorder.com</u>.

> Honorée Enterprises Publishing, LLC
> <u>Honoree@HonoreeCorder.com</u>
> <u>HonoreeCorder.com</u>
> <u>https://www.linkedin.com/in/honoree/</u>
> Twitter: @honoree
> Instagram: @empirebuilderusa
> Facebook: https://www.facebook.com/Honoree